LIFE SENTENCE AT STAMFORD BRIDGE

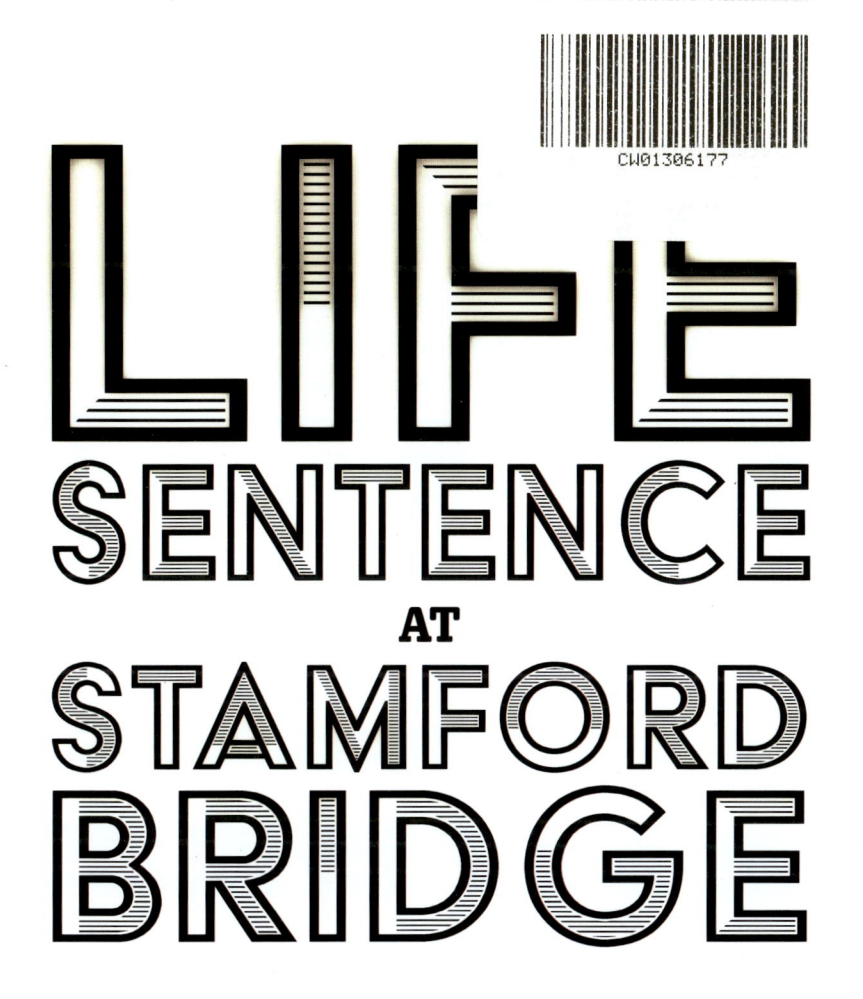

Live from Stamford Bridge Since 1993

JAMIE STREET

Copyright © 2018 by Jamie Street

All rights reserved. This book or any portion thereof may not be reproduced or used in any manner whatsoever without the express written permission of the publisher except for the use of brief quotations in a book review. This book and its contents are in no way supported or affiliated with Chelsea Football Club. All views and perspectives are the author's personal opinion and perspective.

https://www.throwbackblues.com

Hi, I'm Jamie.

The one in the middle in case you are wondering. That's me, my Dad (left) and my Grandad (right) celebrating Chelsea's first trophy in over 25 years. A historic FA Cup win at the "Old Wembley". 2-0 against Middlesborough in 1997. Chelsea Legend Roberto Di-matteo with a goal in 43 seconds. What a day!

2018 marks the 25th year that I have had the pleasure of going to support my club, Chelsea FC at Stamford Bridge. From a 1-1 draw at home to Sheffield Wednesday in 1993, to the everlasting high of European glory of Munich in 2012. 25 years has been packed with incredible highs, lows and unforgettable memories. So often, I look back on those afternoons, nights, European adventures and the memories deliver a huge surge of happiness, nostalgia and pride.

The memories of supporting Chelsea has inspired me to start my blog "Throwback Blues" and write this book recollecting incredible occasions at Stamford Bridge.

Jamie Street

West Stand Lower - Block 5

This book is dedicated to:

My Grandad,

a lifelong Chelsea fan who inspired our family to follow Chelsea.

My Dad,

who has shared these experiences with me for the past 25 years.

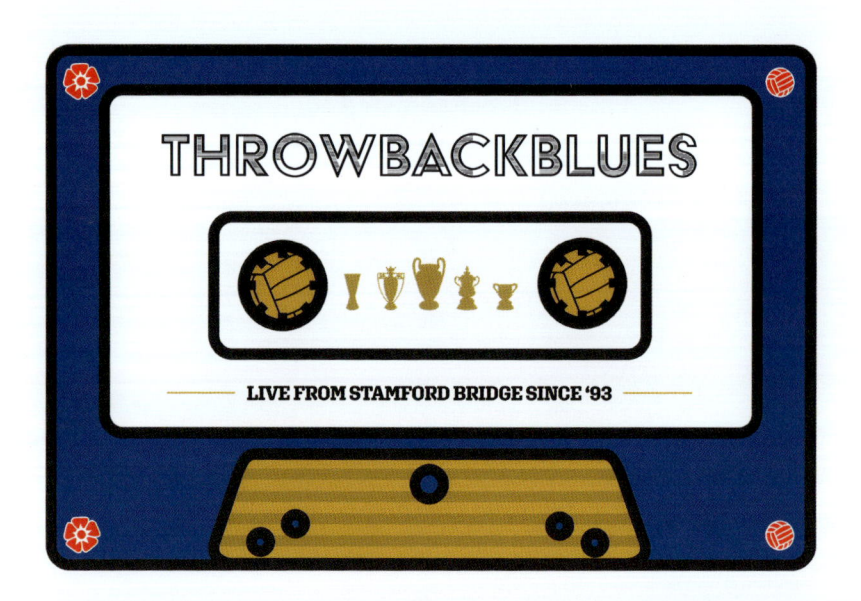

THROWBACKBLUES

LIVE FROM STAMFORD BRIDGE SINCE '93

www.throwbackblues.com

LIFE SENTENCE AT STAMFORD BRIDGE

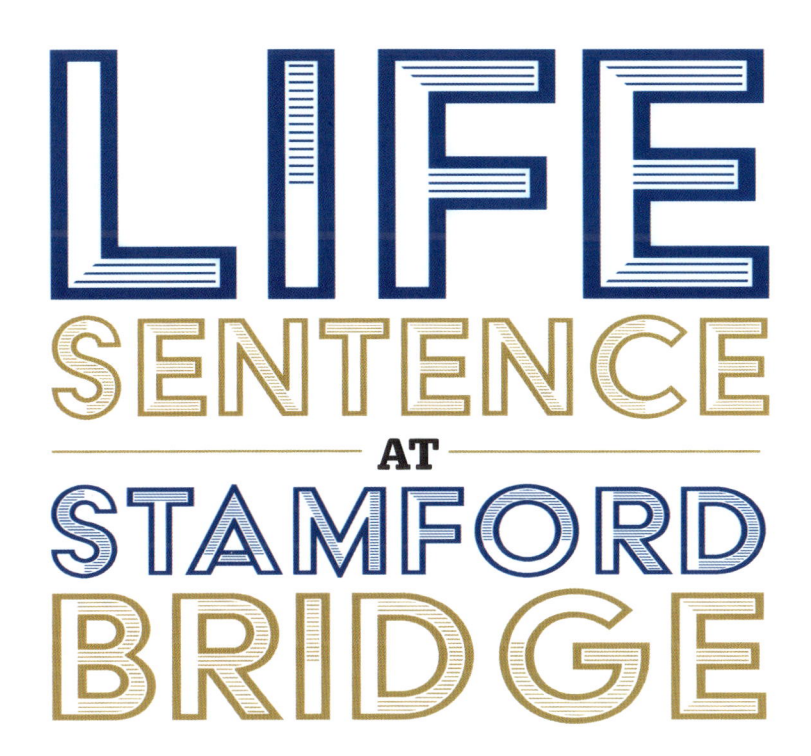

CONTENTS

- **INTRODUCTION** — 6
- **FIRST DAY AT THE BRIDGE** — 7
- **GREATEST PREMIER LEAGUE GAMES** — 10
- **STAMFORD BRIDGE'S BEST PLAYERS** — 30
- **GREATEST CUP GAMES** — 50
- **TOP 10 CHELSEA MANAGERS** — 68
- **THE ROLLERCOASTER TO MUNICH** — 81

INTRODUCTION

If Stamford Bridge is a prison, lock me up and throw away the key. Since being omitted into my seat in 1993, I've enjoyed some of the most incredible moments of my life sitting next to my Dad. At the age of 30, it is perfect timing for me to look back and reflect on 25 very very special years, to gather my thoughts and appreciate what it means to be a Chelsea fan. Sharing how it felt to have the privilege of watching Chelsea deliver a rollercoaster of emotions into our lives.
I look forward to taking you on my blue journey and reliving these incredible memories once again.

FIRST DAY AT THE BRIDGE

LIVE FROM STAMFORD BRIDGE SINCE '93

Chelsea V Sheffield Wednesday
Saturday 28th August 1993

The first day at the Bridge, is a day a five year old doesn't forget. I remember a mass of people going in to the ground, the sight of the stadium ahead, thousands of people packed into one area shouting, cheering, swearing. Navigating this situation physically and mentally was the first challenge of the day. I was emotionally exhausted before a ball had been kicked. I still remember the rotating turnstiles at Stamford Bridge, handing over my ticket to have the stub removed and sitting in the East Stand Upper next to my Dad. The smell of the ground in 1993 still endures, with the concoction of cigars and beer hanging in the air. Whenever I smell a cigar on a different occasion I can't help but think of the Stamford Bridge East Stand.

I spent most of the time standing on my seat when anything happened. As a little lad it wasn't easy to keep hoisting myself up on to the seat without thinking you were going to fall over. As a result I missed our goal, David Lee scoring to cancel out a Mark Bright opener for Sheffield Wednesday. Not seeing the goal didn't really matter, the reaction

1 man and his dog spot went to mow a meadow
one man and his dog spot went to mow a meadow

2 men and his dog spot went to mow a meadow
two men and his dog spot went to mow a meadow

3 men and his dog spot went to mow a meadow
three men and his dog spot went to mow a meadow

4 men and his dog spot went to mow a meadow
five men and his dog spot went to mow a meadow

5 men and his dog spot went to mow a meadow
four men and his dog spot went to mow a meadow

6 men and his dog spot went to mow a meadow
six men and his dog spot went to mow a meadow

7 men and his dog spot went to mow a meadow
seven men and his dog spot went to mow a meadow

8 men and his dog spot went to mow a meadow
eight men and his dog spot went to mow a meadow

9 men and his dog spot went to mow a meadow
nine men and his dog spot went to mow a meadow

10 men went to mow!
went to mow a meadow!
one man and his dog spot,
went to mow a meadow!

CHELSEA! CHELSEA! CHELSEA!

around me told me something had happened. My ears and eyes told me. I was just trying to cope with the incredible noise and scenes of people jumping around in celebration. At that age your senses hadn't been exposed to those volumes and it was kind of scary to hear something so loud and people throwing their arms and pumping their fists almost uncontrollably. The game ended 1-1. It was frightening, but at the same time electric. It was that feeling that would keep me coming back for a further 25 years, feeling uncontrollably alive in the moment of celebration.

I have massive envy for anyone attending their first Chelsea match in the coming days, weeks or months. The new emotions you will discover, the smells, the songs, the sights. It brings a shiver down my spine just thinking of how it would feel to live that moment again. All the little components that make up that first visit to Stamford Bridge.

The first Chelsea match is undoubtedly a special one, but this book is 25 years in the making. A reflection of the most memorable experiences as a willing prisoner at Stamford Bridge. Scintillating Saturday and Sunday afternoons, epic European nights under the lights at Stamford Bridge as some of the finest football players on the planet provide entertainment beyond imagination. The beautiful game at the Bridge is brought back to life through the eyes of one boy who became a man with blue blood running through his veins.

I hope you have as much fun reading this book as I did living these magical moments.

GREATEST PREMIER LEAGUE GAMES

LIVE FROM STAMFORD BRIDGE SINCE '93

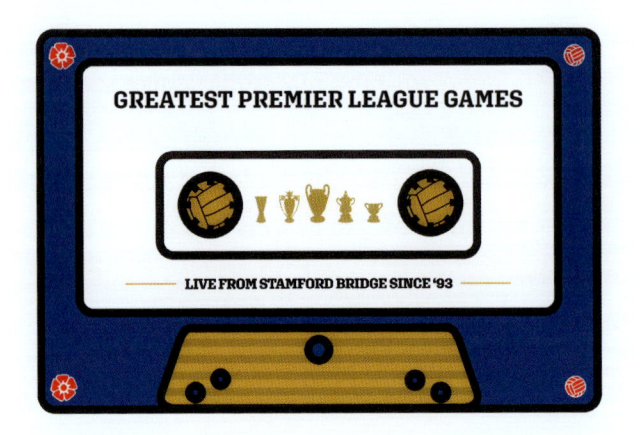

Unlike today the Premier League has not always been a place where Chelsea are fighting at the the top of the table. There have been darker times, different divisions and less belief in a blue tomorrow. During my era as a Chelsea fan I have been extremely lucky to witness a monumental shift in fortune, both on and off the pitch.

Even before the introduction of Roman Abramovich, during the 1995/96 pre-season a new era at Stamford Bridge was beginning to form. The Manager at the time Glenn Hoddle signed Dutch superstar Ruud Gullit from Sampdoria that would have untold influence on Chelsea's future. I remember watching the news at my Grans in the New Forest when it was first announced. These were long before the days of instant news sources such as websites and social media. It was a massive signing for Chelsea.

Ruud Gullit would pave the way for the introduction of even more foreign investment, leading to the likes of Gianfranco Zola, Roberto Di Matteo and Gianluca Vialli. Those players would guide the club to multiple domestic and European success' that had not been experienced since the early 1970's.

In the season 1998/98 we came extremely close to being Champions finishing 3rd only 4 points Champions Manchester United. The early 2000's we would continue to be a top side competing for the top six positions, but it wasn't until the arrival of Roman Abramovich in 2003 that we suddenly became a force continuously in contention for top honours. The following fifteen years would provide five Premier League trophies amongst a treasure chest of domestic and European silverware.

As I am frequently reminded my journey as a Chelsea fan at Stamford Bridge has been one of absolute privilege and greed in the grand scheme of Chelsea's overall history. As much as I'd like to take the plaudits, I have to remind my Dad it's a coincidence I have been able to enjoy such levels of success. Here are my favourite games from Chelsea's ventures in the top flight at Stamford Bridge.

2005   2006   2010   2015   2017

CHELSEA 4
BLACKBURN 0
Gudjohnsen (37, 38, 51) Duff (74)
Saturday 23rd October, 2004

A personal choice finds its place in my rendition of the all time greatest Chelsea games. At the time it was a relatively straight forward 4-0 victory against Blackburn, but Eidur Gudjohnsen scoring his first hat-trick for Chelsea made it extra special for me. When I was 17, Gudjohnsen was my stand out Chelsea hero, and had been for a few years prior to that season. His clever link up play, elegance on and off the ball, finishing ability and the greatest goal celebration ever, made him a player I admired. He was a class act.

Gudjohnsen only played 70 minutes of the game, but it was enough time for him to score his very first hat-trick for the club. It was a stroll in the park victory at a very rainy Stamford Bridge, with Eidur picking up two of his goals inside two first half minutes and claiming his hat-trick from the penalty spot early in the second. Compared to some of the other players at the club during the 2004 season, Drogba, Lampard, Robben, Duff and Joe Cole there were frequent question marks over what Gudjohnsen actually offered. He wasn't as prolific as he had been during his partnership with Hasselbaink in previous seasons and there were lot of question marks over his contribution.

This hat-trick and on various other occasions during that title winning season he proved his value. As a massive Gudjohnsen fan it was great to see him grab the headlines and reinstate his value to the team.

CHELSEA 5
MANCHESTER UNITED 0
Chris Sutton (16), Gus Poyet (54, 1), Berg (59 og), J Morris (81)
Sunday 3rd October, 1999

The late 1990's was a period where you simply didn't expect to get a result against Manchester United. Chants of you "Only came for United" were frequently sung from the away end, whilst Chelsea fans naturally responded with "You only live round the corner". Times have changed somewhat today, the "Manchester" faithful are more likely to be chanting "where were you when you were…" in response to us beating them. Our response hasn't changed too much, other than perhaps mentioning their decline in the wake of their City rivals.

Nonetheless, back in 1999 something truly unheard of happened: Chris Sutton scored a Premier League goal in a Chelsea shirt. That was enough to make headlines in itself as the big summer signing from Blackburn failed to live up to high expectations during a single season at the Club. Side story aside, Chris Sutton's goal would be the spark to a famous 5-0 victory for Chelsea against the incredible force that was Manchester United. Two goals from Gus Poyet, an own goal and a late finish from the Chelsea Youth Team and Derby Country Assistant Coach of recent times Jody Morris would go down as one of the most emphatic and memorable victories of recent times. Yes we had lifted three trophies across the two previous seasons, but not by beating opposition of Manchester United's calibre and standing. This was a truly special occasion for Chelsea fans who were largely unfamiliar with this success. The 5-0 demolition of Manchester United came as a small ounce of revenge for the 4-0 defeat we had suffered in the FA Cup Final of 1994. Beating Manchester United in todays era is still a great experience, beating them back then left you feeling on top of the world.

CHELSEA 3
TOTTENHAM HOTSPUR 1
Gullit (27), Lee (52, pen), Di Matteo (80)
Saturday 26th October 1996

The memory of this match is less about the victory and more about the events surrounding it. In the week before, Matthew Harding lifelong Chelsea fan and investor had lost his life during a Helicopter crash whilst returning from a mid-week match against Bolton.

As an eight year old, the scenes of emotions and support for Matthew Harding were of huge significance. The feeling of the entire club coming together to thank and remember him for his support and impact on Chelsea Football Club. Of course Matthew Harding's name is an ever present at Stamford Bridge, with the North stand being named the "Matthew Harding Stand" and chants of "Matthew Harding's Blue and White Army" frequently heard from the Chelsea faithful. This was my first real experience of this type of community and belonging that being a Chelsea fan offered and has lived long in the memory in terms of Stamford Bridge being more than a place to go and watch Chelsea play football. Chelsea would win the match against close rivals Tottenham, but the match will always be seen as a turning point for Football having a purpose beyond beating rivals and winning games, it could bring people together.

GOAL ALERT!

Hazard vs.. Arsenal (Saturday 4th February 2017)

When you watch a goal like Eden Hazard's against Arsenal in 2017 in real time, it's difficult to comprehend what you have just seen. You forget this is a *"human"* who has picked up the ball close to the halfway

Carefree wherever you may be, we are the famous CFC, we don't give a stuff, whoever you may be 'cause we are the famous...

CFC!

www.throwbackblues.com

line, brushing off a defender intent on stopping him in his tracks no matter the cost, instead of falling to the ground under the pressure the "*human*" would continue to run towards the Arsenal goal, surely he will pass the ball, but no a drop of the shoulder and another defender is beaten, and then with very little of the goal to aim at chips the ball over the oncoming keeper. A truly incredible goal, that gets better every time you watch it.

CHELSEA 4
NEWCASTLE 0
Lampard (63), Drogba (69), Robben (89), Kezman (90, pen)
Saturday 4th December 2004

The December fixture against Newcastle proved to be a significant one in the Club's challenge towards its first Championship title in 50 years. We had started the season strongly, with only a single defeat in the opening 15 games and coming off a 4-0 win away to Charlton, we were top of the league. The opening half of the game suggested otherwise. A promising start to the campaign, and an attitude that Newcastle would come to Stamford Bridge and lay down. Little consideration for the fact they had been in the top five in the previous two seasons. Something happened at half time and its name was Didier Drogba. His introduction to the team would result in a flood of goals all of which would come in the final 30 minutes. An emphatic 4-0 victory, was exhilarating and created genuine belief that this team had what it took to dig deep and deliver. A skill that was essential if we were to maintain a charge towards the title throughout the season.

It will always be a game I will remember for Didier Drogba stepping up to be the man for the big moment. A role he would thrive in throughout the next decade. His celebration after scoring Chelsea's second in the

69th minute and shouting at the Matthew Harding stand "I'm Back!" was the start of a long standing relationship with the fans. The "Drogba Legend" was just beginning.

GOAL ALERT!

Essien vs. Barcelona (Wednesday 6th May 2009)

The spectacle of Michael Essien's stunning strike is overshadowed by a series of events during the match that have prevented it from being considered the greatest goal ever at Stamford Bridge. For all fans that were at Stamford Bridge that evening or watching on the Television you know exactly what I am talking about. Following a 0-0 draw in the Nou Camp, Chelsea were keen to clinch the win that would see us progress through to a second successive Champions League final and opportunity to gain revenge over Manchester United. In the eighth minute of this epic clash, the ball would pop up relatively harmlessly in the direction of Michael Essien who was 35 yards from the goal. An instinctive swing of the left boot would send the ball flying high, like a thunderbolt it would come crashing down onto the underside of the crossbar and into the Barcelona net. A truly incredible strike, that would give us the advantage. As a Chelsea fan in the stadium, we began to to believe this was finally our year.

CHELSEA 4
MANCHESTER UNITED 0
Pedro (1), Cahill (21), Eden Hazard (62), Kante (72)
Sunday 23rd October 2016

Chelsea's credentials were in question before this epic tie against Manchester United in 2016 at Stamford Bridge. Despite picking up two wins against teams we were expected to beat it was the two defeats before to Arsenal and Liverpool that had really punctured any aspirations for the title or even the top 4 that season. As a fan there was an overarching feel of damage limitation and uncertainty surrounding one of the biggest games of the season.

Many questions were being asked of Manager Antonio Conte and facing a team of Manchester United's magnitude would place his position at the club under even greater scrutiny. It came at a time that Conte's inspirational 3-5-2 lacked the appreciation that he received in the months to follow.

To thicken the plot even further it was the return of our "Special One" Jose Mourinho as the Manager of Manchester United that seemed to set Stamford Bridge beyond boiling point before a ball had been kicked. Despite guiding us to three Premier League titles, 2 Carling Cups and an FA Cup, he was now in the dug-out of one our fiercest rivals.

Stamford Bridge wasn't given the opportunity to simmer down as inside the 1st minute, a lapse in the United defence would allow Pedro to fire home and trigger Stamford Bridge to quite simply erupt. All the build-up and media talk exploded in a roar of blue emotion. I feel sorry for anyone who arrived late to that game.

Conte's energy on the touchline would orchestrate the Stormy Stamford

Cesc Fabregas is magic,
he wears a magic hat,
he could have gone to Arsenal,
but he said no stuff that.
he passes with his left foot,
he passes with his right,
and when we win the league again,
we'll sing this song all night!

The scum from Spurs,
they bought his flight,
but Willian, he saw the light,
he got the call from Ambramovich,
and off he went to Stamford Bridge,
he hates Tottenham,
he hates Tottenham
he hates Tottenham,
and he hates Tottenham!

Bridge crowd, and a second soon followed thanks to Gary Cahill being in the box at the right place at the right time. Manchester United had their chances, but it was another fast passing move and a great piece of trickery from Eden Hazard that would ensure another Stamford Bridge eruption an hour into the game. The finishing touch to a volcanic victory at the Bridge was provided by Kante, who weaved his way into the box majestically and put the ball passed De Gea in goal with 20 minutes still left to play. The fans were in party mode and a wave of new found belief was beginning to bubble up around Stamford Bridge. People should know by now, never write off Chelsea.

CHELSEA 2
TOTTENHAM 1
Essien (14), Gallas (90)
Saturday 11ᵗʰ March 2006

The ability to dig deep was the underlying lesson that fans learnt from this hard fought victory against Tottenham in 2006. A month had passed since suffering an eye-opening 3-0 defeat away to Middlesbrough and despite making amends in the two games that followed, the visit of a strong Tottenham team suggested the Premier League trophy was not guaranteed to stay at Stamford Bridge for another season.

My confidence that we would win the league again was reflected by the fact I had purchased the new Chelsea shirt for the 2005/06 season with "CHAMPIONS 06" printed on the back even before a ball had been kicked that season. A crazy thing to do and one I would never do again, simply because I think too much now. Despite another 12 years of success I know how quickly the Football environment can change from one year to the next. Chelsea fans can take the fall from Champions in 2015 to 10th the year after as a perfect example.

A first half stoppage time equaliser from Jenas for Tottenham cancelled out Frank Lampard's strike earlier in the half, leaving the sides level at the break. The second half proved be an extremely frustrating one and Jose Mourinho's famous phrase of "parking the bus" was likely to feature in his after match press conference.

Despite countless attacks being thwarted by Spurs stubborn defence, there was still time for William Gallas, an unlikely hero to find space on the edge of the box and hammer home emphatically following uncharacteristic surge past two Tottenham defenders. The importance of the 94th minute goal was apparent from the players who celebrated wildly on the touchline with the Manager, their efforts rewarded for never giving up.

The satisfaction of scoring so late on to win a game always trumps a straight forward multiple goal victory, but to do so against one of your biggest London rivals and keep our Championship hopes firmly on track thickened the roar that reverberated around Stamford Bridge that afternoon. My wildly optimistic "CHAMPIONS 06" Chelsea shirt was still very much a wise investment for now at least.

GOAL ALERT!
Lampard vs. Bayern Munich (Wednesday 6th April 2005)
The Stamford Bridge flood lights were not the only source of light on this very special European night. In the 70th minute of this massive clash against German giants Bayern Munich a beacon of Chelsea blue would glow brightly. Frank Lampard would take a difficult ball high on his chest, his control would put the ball seemingly behind him and impossible to shoot. Frank had other ideas, swivelling quickly and instant-

ly smashing the ball passed the Bayern Goalkeeper and into the net. A technically incredible finish, on the biggest stage. To add to the quality of the goal, Bayern goalkeeper Kahn wasn't just any goalkeeper, he was considered one of the best in the world. As the German International goalkeeper it felt particularly special for Englishman Frank Lampard to smash the ball past him with such expertise. Super Frank Lampard had served up a sensational strike, sending the Stamford Bridge faithful into absolute raptures.

CHELSEA 6
ARSENAL 0

Eto'o (5), Schürrle (7), E Hazard (17), Oscar (42, 66), Salah (71)
Saturday 22nd March 2014

Since setting foot inside Stamford Bridge in 1993, it became apparent that Arsenal were a team we simply didn't beat. For over a decade they were the team you never felt safe against. Winterburn's last minute free kick would claim a 3-2 victory for Arsenal at the Bridge in 1997. A 2-0 lead in 1999, would be overturned by a 15 minute hat-trick from Kanu, and despite taking a 1-0 lead in the first minute in 2003/04 they would go on to win comfortably 2-1. The cups would provide a minor reprieve, but we still suffered in the 2002 FA Cup despite dominating much of that game. Arsenal were a team that would leave you having nightmares season after season. It wasn't until the 2005/06 season we would break the curse and enjoy more frequent victories against our London rivals. Chelsea have claimed more silverware success than Arsenal over recent years, but they have still remained an extremely tough opponent. These memories made the match in March 2014 all that more enjoyable.

This London derby would be Arsene Wenger's 1000th game as the Arsenal Manager. He was the man behind the teams that had stolen our hopes and dreams throughout the 1990's and early 2000's. Whilst some degree of revenge had been delivered between times, there was a massive degree of satisfaction in delivering a nightmare to Wenger he would never forget.

Inside five minutes we were a goal ahead through Eto'o, seven minutes 2-0 through Schurrle, 3-0 after 17 minutes thanks to Hazard from the penalty spot. Oscar would grab a goal either side of half time and Salah would score in the 71st to leave us 6-0 ahead with still over 20 minutes to play, no concerns over a later come back on this occasion! The game would end 6-0. Such was the way the game unravelled, with the ball hitting the back of the net so freely, there was an overwhelming desire from the fans for more goals. Despite coming into the game with the view that "*any win will do*", humiliation was now high on the agenda. Memories of the last minute heartbreaks were now long forgotten, London was blue. Given the history surrounding the fixture and the bragging rights at stake, it was a momentous victory that deserves to go down as one of the greatest ever at Stamford Bridge

CHELSEA 2
LIVERPOOL 1

Desailly (13), Gronkjaer (26)
Sunday 11th May 2003

There are many things to love about this fixture against Liverpool. Its significance would have monumental influence on Chelsea Football Club. On the surface it was a game against one of the biggest clubs in the country. On closer inspection it was a game that would decide who would qualify for the following season's Champions League. The importance of that fact was even greater for Chelsea who were in a precarious financial position.

The game didn't start well with Liverpool taking the lead early on through Hypia, leaving them in pole position to take the final place in Europe's elite competition. Goals before half time from World Cup Winner Marcel Desailly and Jesper Gronkjaer turned the tie on its head. One of the fondest memories was Gianfranco Zola's cameo skills in the corner flag that left Jamie Carragher on the floor as the Italian magician ran down the clock. It was to be Zola's last game for Chelsea and it was fitting that he would show every ounce of the sparkle that he had brought to club since his arrival in 1996. Twisting and turning unlike any other striker on the brink of his 37th Birthday, brought back memories of his iconic goal against West Ham in 1996, and his stunning strike in the semi final of the 1997 FA Cup against Wimbledon. A true Chelsea legend. The game would end 2-1 and Champions League football would return to Stamford Bridge the following season in addition to a degree of greater financial stability.

Little did we know the following summer Russian billionaire Roman Abramovich would buy Chelsea FC and supercharge Chelsea's positive trajectory towards the English and European elite. Without clinching victory against Liverpool on the final day of the season, Chelsea's future would have taken a significantly different course. Who knows what I would have written about if that had been the case!

A special day to be at Stamford Bridge as fans celebrated the superstar of previous seasons provide the path for a new team of heroes to continue his work. The Italian had built the foundations for a blue empire and era of dominance beyond every fans imagination.

CHELSEA 3
MANCHESTER UNITED 0
Gallas (5), J Cole (61), Carvalho (73)
Saturday 29th April 2006

Can you imagine a better way of clinching the title than beating Manchester United 3-0? Needing only a point to seal back-to-back Premier League victories a rampant Chelsea would go on and do just that.

An early goal from Gallas would set the team on their way and an incredible solo effort from Joe Cole would all but confirm the most coveted silverware would remain in the Chelsea cabinet for another season. Carvalho even got in on the act 10 minutes later to confirm a hard fought victory.

Aside from the achievement, the game panned out in such a way that Stamford Bridge could begin to celebrate just beyond the hour mark. Any tension surrounding a defeat that could lead to the Championship going to Old Trafford instead had been eliminated and Chelsea fans could begin to bask in glory. Such was our superiority in '05/'06 sea-

We are going to win the league, *AGAIN!*
we are going to win the league, *AGAIN!*
Now you can believe us, now you can believe us, now you can belive ussssss we are going to win the league...*AGAIN!*

2005   2006

www.throwbackblues.com

son it seemed unlikely we would sacrifice a successive Premier league trophy, even if we had been been beaten. For that reason clinching the title against Manchester United doesn't claim the top spot as the greatest game at Stamford Bridge. Nevertheless it doesn't take anything away from the magnitude of the achievement and experience. To comfortably beat Manchester United and then lift the Premier League trophy in front of them, that was a genuine statement that Chelsea are here to stay.

GOAL ALERT!

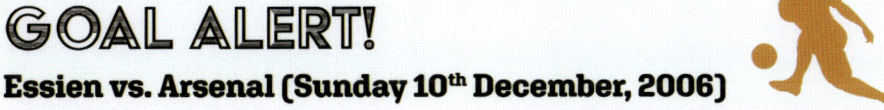

Essien vs. Arsenal (Sunday 10th December, 2006)

The 2006/07 season was a period where the Stamford Bridge faithful were simply unfamiliar with defeat. Jose Mourinho had built his fortress and for a team to come away with victory was unheard of. To fall behind on the 78th minute to a Flamini strike suggested that run was about to come to an end, and against our close London rivals of all teams. In the 84th minute Michael Essien had other ideas. Thirty five yards from the goal the ball would roll into his path, perfectly positioned for a strike with his weaker left foot Essien swung with his right making perfect contact with the outside of his boot. The ball exploded from his foot and players and fans could only watch as it almost ripped the net away from the goal posts. An incredible goal and the home record remained intact.

CHELSEA 8
WIGAN 0

Anelka (6), Lampard (32 pen), Kalou (54), Anelka (56), Drogba (63, 68 pen, 80), A Cole (90)
Sunday 9th May 2010

This is the greatest game ever at Stamford Bridge. To truly capture the magnitude of this game and its rightful position as the best ever, It requires a recap of the seasons events. Early in 2010, we would lose to Jose Mourinho's Inter Milan and be eliminated from the Champions League. Followed by an underwhelming 1-1 draw away to Blackburn. According to many Chelsea were a spent force, silverware was unlikely to be added to the cabinet this season.

An incredible run of results would accumulate to the most glorious of outcomes. 5-0 away against Portsmouth, 7-1 at home against Aston Villa, a 2-1 win at Old Trafford that would turn the title race in our favour, a 7-0 win at the Bridge over Stoke and a 2-0 win at Anfield would pave the way for a nail biting final game of the season at Stamford Bridge. Despite so may emphatic victories, our lead over Manchester United was a single point.

The week building up to that game would conjure up all the permutations of winning, losing or drawing. There was so much tension and expectation around and inside the ground on that day. We all knew that any win would do, but could we emotionally handle the situation?
From a personal perspective the season decider holds even greater meaning. My Grandad a lifelong Chelsea fan had recently passed away. There were personal memories and experiences that were present before and throughout that game. I knew that my Dad in particular was finding

the situation hard to manage. Generally a relatively unemotional figure, I could see how mixed emotions and elements of grief were weighing heavily on him. I was also feeling the loss of my Grandad, but the hardest thing for me was imagining how my Dad felt. To be in his shoes, and thinking how it would feel for me to prepare for a potential Chelsea celebration knowing that my Dad wasn't there to enjoy it with us was unthinkable. My Grandad was a frequent visitor to Stamford Bridge well before my time at the club, his hero's such as Roy Bentley were from the Championship team of 1955. My Grandad was the inspiration behind us all supporting Chelsea, and for him not be able to watch and enjoy this was difficult to handle.

Anelka gave us the lead early on and Lampard scored from the spot to give us a strong 2-0 lead going into the second half. A blitz of 6 goals including a 17 minute hat trick from Drogba would emphatically confirm Chelsea as Champions of England once again. However, It was the scenes that followed Nicola Anelka's second goal on 56 minutes that truly underpinned this game as the greatest game to be a Chelsea fan in the stadium at that time. With over 30 minutes left to play and 4-0 ahead the celebrations could start early. All of the tension and anxiety that had been bottled up burst into scenes of blue and white as cheers of champions echoed around the Stadium. "The bouncy" was in full flow and there was even enough time to sing every players name.

It was in this moment that I knew my Dad was struggling the most, struggling to come to terms with the confused mixture of happy and sad emotions. All I could do was turn to him and say was *"they did it for Grandad"*.

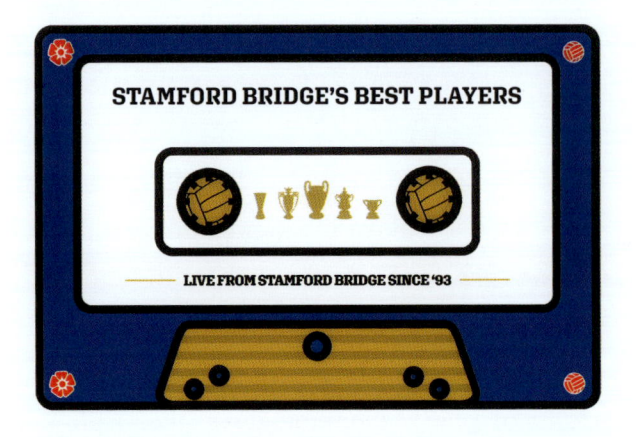

STAMFORD BRIDGE'S BEST PLAYERS

LIVE FROM STAMFORD BRIDGE SINCE '93

To say we have been blessed with super star talent at Stamford Bridge since I first set foot in the ground in 1993 is a bit of an understatement. The hallowed turf at Stamford Bridge might as well be considered a blue carpet (red is banned), that has hosted many of the worlds best week after week. Players that have scored goals to help deliver success, provided incredible spectacle through speed and trickery, dominant leadership to lift the club through the toughest periods and the safest hands to carry the confidence of the team on their shoulders. Simply selecting ten of the best from such a spectrum would appear to be an impossible task, but by taking into account the importance of each player in Chelsea's history I have taken up the challenge.

GOAL ALERT!

Gallas vs. Tottenham (Sunday 17th September 2006)

With the game heading for a frustrating 1-1 draw and points lost in the title race, William Gallas would take destiny into his own right foot. Ninety plus four minutes on the clock, and with seemingly no space to work with out on the left wing, he would worm his way across the edge of the box and crack a speculative effort through the Spurs defenders and beyond the outreaching keeper. Stamford Bridge shook. The manager and players went wild. 2-1 Chelsea. Three points.

ASHLEY COLE
FROM: 2006-2014

When Ashley Cole arrived from Arsenal after an extended transfer saga in 2006, it was hard to imagine him becoming one of Chelsea's greatest players. Firstly, he was a *"Gooner"* who was widely documented as signing for Chelsea just for the money. Secondly we lost William Gallas in the process, who had been one of our best players in recent years and was very much a blue. Cole would go on to prove himself on the pitch time and time again and despite it taking a significant number of years before the fans took to him, Ashley Cole would become a *"true blue"*. The transition from red to blue can sometimes take a bit of time, especially if the media want to make it as difficult as possible for that transition to take place.

It was was his consistent high level performances that made him such a valued player at the Bridge. His ability to stop even the worlds best such as Cristiano Ronaldo and Lionel Messi showcased his defensive talents. His attacking cross capability made him the complete left back, with so many others in his position only able to excel in one department. Whilst playing for Chelsea Ashley Cole won the Premier League with in 2010, three FA Cups, the European Cup and the UEFA Cup.

A defining moment for me and for many was when he stood up to take a penalty in the 2012 Champions League final in Munich. With a wall of Bayern Munich fans behind the goal encouraging him to miss, he planted the ball in the bottom right corner and kept the dream alive for Chelsea fans around the world. Ashley Cole's legendary status was confirmed as we went on to lift the trophy (*"Ashley Cole's Won the European Cup!"*).

RUUD GULLIT
FROM: 1995-1998

As a seven year old the arrival of Ruud Gullit at Chelsea is one I remember with great fondness. News emerged in the Summer of 1995 via a thing called the Television. No internet or social media to rely on then. Signing this type of player was a massive achievement for the club at the time. Unlike today where we are frequently associated with the top players and having a star studded line up is second nature, Chelsea were a team that simply didn't attract players of Ruud Gullit's pedigree at that time.

He joined Chelsea following a hugely successful club and international career, he was a winner and player that brought a style of *"sexy football"* that Stamford Bridge had not seen for some time. In many respects he was the initial seed that inspired years of success at Stamford Bridge, on the field he would effortlessly create space, have incredible range of passing, fantastic strength and have the ability to score from in and outside the box. Admittedly his arrival only came two years after my first game at Chelsea, but his class shone through immediately. Signing him as a player would lead to his future Managerial position, and the introduction of even more foreign talent that would set us on our way to our first piece of silverware for over a quarter of a century. A player of Ruud Gullit's calibre may be expected to arrive through the doors at Stamford Bridge today, but his importance to Chelsea in the mid 90's should never be undervalued which warrants his inclusion as one of Chelsea' best ever.

You are my Chelsea
my only Chelsea,
 you make me happy
when skies are grey

You will never know how,
much I love you
 until you have taken
my Chelsea away!

You are my Chelsea
my only Chelsea,
 you make me happy
when skies are grey

You will never know how
much I love you
 until you have taken
my Chelsea away!

www.throwbackblues.com

MARCEL DESAILLY
FROM: 1998-2004

In Marcel Desailly Chelsea had gained the services of a World Cup Winner in 1998. His stature in world football was significant and it was immediate to opposing teams the value of a player of his capability would bring to Stamford Bridge. It was his positional sense, technical ability and intelligence that made him such an important part of the Chelsea team. It was in Desailly's first season that we would claim 3rd place and qualify for the Champions League, we were only 4 points off of top spot. For me Marcel Desailly is what made Chelsea a Champions League calibre club. For all the attacking qualities we had, his partnership with Frank Leboeuf made for far more balanced team. With Desailly in the side you felt confident that Chelsea would be capable of keeping a clean sheet or closing out a game to gain valuable draws and wins that would make the difference at the end of the season. His knowledge, expertise and leadership skills (as Chelsea captain) would also prove to be pivotal in John Terry's progression to become one of the best central defenders in Europe.

CLAUDE MAKELELE
FROM: 2003-2008

Amongst an influx of spectacle names at Chelsea during the period after 2003, no one expected Claude Makelele to prove to be the essential puzzle piece that would enable Chelsea to become a super force in Football. Makelele enjoyed two premier league success' at Chelsea in addition to an FA Cup and two League Cups. He was the unspoken one, who went about his business relieving the pressure on the defence and enabling the creative players in front of him to perform at their highest level. He was never one to set the stadium alight with a magical bit of skill, instead he was instrumental in ensuring we were stable at the back and incredibly dangerous on the attack. As a kid he was a player that I would try to emulate the most, watching from the Stamford Bridge stands I always tried to learn from the way he played. Players of this type are so often the difference between two great teams, both may feature great forwards and attacking talents but the team without a Makelele would find it extremely difficult to get the most from them. Makelele is a treasure of a player.

Such was his impact in English Football, fans and the media would refer to his role as the "Makelele" role for many years even after his departure. In years to come N'Golo Kante may be considered an even greater evolution of Makelele, given his ability to protect the defence but also cover significant distance but for now Makelele is still the king of the deep lying midfielder and a massive influence on a team that hadn't won a league title for fifty years.

EDEN HAZARD
FROM: 2012-PRESENT

Unlike all the other players that populate this list, Eden Hazard is the only name that features on Chelsea's team sheet today. That's not to say that other current players aren't good enough, it's just a case of at the time of writing they don't do quite enough to make the top 10 in my view. The fact that Eden Hazard features truly is a sentiment to his ability and overall importance to the club. In terms of raw talent and technical skillset, Hazard is arguably the greatest player to wear the blue shirt at Stamford Bridge. His ability to beat multiple players at all speeds even places him above Gianfranco Zola in that department. His talent is so high, that it is only a similarly short player, Lionel Messi from Barcelona that is may be more mesmerising to watch. Hazard still has some way to go before he reaches those heights on a world level, but his impact and development since his arrival at Chelsea in the summer 2012 cannot go unnoticed. He has produced so many moments of incredible spectacle. Not least, his unbelievable solo run and goal against Arsenal in the 2016/17 Premier League winning season. Scoring big goals in big games is a hallmark of his hero status, the winning goal from the penalty spot in the 2018 FA Cup Final against Manchester United, the goal that clinched the title against Crystal Palace in 2015 and the incredible finish against Tottenham that handed Leicester the Premier League title in 2016.

There have been so many moments of individual quality and team build up play that justify Hazard's star status. As a fan watching him play week in week out it is a luxury that's hard to appreciate from inside the ground, you almost take it for granted. It's not until you read about him, talk about him with supporters of other clubs and see him play for Belgium that you realise how much of a talent we have at Chelsea. With Hazard featured in the team, Chelsea stand to achieve even greater success and with it Eden's legendary status will only get bigger.

GIANFRANCO ZOLA
FROM: 1996-2003

In terms of ability on the ball Gianfranco Zola provided a spectacle to Stamford Bridge that I had never seen at Chelsea. Nine at the time and with little knowledge of him as a player I wasn't sure what to expect on his arrival in November 1996. He joined at similar time to many other foreign players including Gianluca Vialli and Roberto Di Matteo as part of Ruud Gullit's significant investment in overseas talent. Little did I know he would provide 7 years of sparkle that would set the club on the path to its most incredible period of success.

From my memory Zola first made his name as a true free-kick specialist, a player with a level of dead ball accuracy unlike any other. I remember a feeling of excitement and expectation inside the ground whenever we got a free kick in and around the box. Zola soon became more to me than a free kick expert following an iconic goal against Manchester United in early 1997, where he walked round the Manchester defence and put the ball effortlessly past Peter Schmeichel. Similar mesmerizing goals would come following outstanding trickery to beat Julian Dicks and

Double, Double, Double!
John Terry has won the double!
while the scum from the lane,
have won nothing again,
John Terry has won the double!

Double, Double, Double!
John Terry has won the double!
while the scum from the lane,
have won nothing again,
John Terry has won the double!

Singing this one on the flight home after the famous night in Munich 2012.
Then and many, many match matchdays at the bridge!

2012

www.throwbackblues.com

score against West Ham, and a pivotal goal in amongst the four goals that overturned a 2-0 deficit against Liverpool in the FA Cup.

The fondest memories I have of Zola at Chelsea came in the 1997 FA Cup Final Semi Final at Highbury against Wimbledon. An incredible turn on the edge of the box, would open the gap to drive home a stunning low finish into the bottom corner, setting us on the way to 3-0 victory and a final at Wembley. Nine at the time it was a magical day of new emotion and immense celebration. The yellow kit we wore that day would also be associated with him and that game. The second memory came in 2002 in an FA Cup fixture against Norwich, it is a fond memory for many Chelsea fans but I remember it so well as it was the last game that I went to Chelsea with my Grandad. A corner from Le Seux and Zola applied a stunning angled mid-air, inside of the boot back flick to guide the ball into the back of the net. A masterclass from the magician even in the later stages of his Chelsea career.

Gianfranco Zola was a hugely important player to Chelsea, he inspired a new style and winning mentality that Chelsea fans had never experienced. He was a genuine driving force behind the fans believing there could be a blue tomorrow. He did more than provide a blue tomorrow, he laid the foundations for a blue era and was a pivotal part in propelling the club from a middle of the table regular to a club fighting for European and domestic league and cup competition.

PETR CECH
FROM: 2004-2015

Petr Cech epitomises the unsung hero. However, for all those that were able to witness his ten years at Chelsea will know that he is simply one of the greatest players to ever wear the shirt and grace the Stamford Bridge turf. His ability to govern defences and provide them with the confidence they needed to perform at their best was just the start of the legacy he would leave at Chelsea. Incredible consistency in goal would lead us to Four Premier League trophies, four FA Cups and three league cups.

However, there were three absolutely defining moments that have cemented his status as a legend in my eyes. The first came in 2006 when Petr somehow came through a life threatening skull fracture sustained via a collision in a match with Reading in 2006. His determination to return, was a sign of incredible courage representative of the Chelsea Lion. Many would have respected his decision to stop playing, but it was his desire and ambition that would take him back to the highest level of football competition. An inspiration to anyone facing fear or uncertainty in life.

Despite multiple Premier League Golden Glove Awards (Most clean sheets in a season) such is the understated value of Cech's role at Chelsea and probably the perception of goalkeepers compared to the goal scorers in taking the headlines, it isn't until 2012 that Petr's star would shine its brightest. The incredible save that Petr Cech made when leading 2-1 in the FA Cup will always be a defining moment for me. His ability to claw the ball off the line from a thunderous Andy Carroll header from six yards remains unbelievable to watch today.

However, Cech's status in the greatest Chelsea players is assured in the Champions League final two weeks after his FA Cup heroics. Three incredible penalty saves, one in extra time from Arjen Robben and the others in the penalty shoot out, were the perfect example of Petr Cech being the unsung hero. Didier Drogba would take the headlines as the goal scorer, but Chelsea fans will never forget the importance of Petr Cech in that final. For many he is the true hero of Munich, and undoubtedly deserves to be considered a Chelsea Legend.

JOHN TERRY
FROM: 1998-2017

"*Captain. Leader. Legend*" are three words that provide sufficient justification for John Terry's inclusion as one of Chelsea's greatest of all time. I have been lucky enough to watch Terry for many of his Seven hundred and seventeen games in a Chelsea career that spans almost 20 years and watched him lead the team to five Premier League trophies, five FA cups, three league cups, a European cup and a UEFA Cup.

As the captain of the team and as a player that continued to prove himself through multiple eras of change and hostility at the club John's legacy speaks for itself. In the moment of that experience, it's hard to see anything beyond a man delivering the same calibre of solid defensive and organisation displays with an incredible number of goals for a player in his position. It's not until you step away from the stands and appreciate the admiration for his playing and leadership abilities from all corners of the football world that you begin to establish his talent. The hatred from opposing fans, simply represented a mark of jealousy and fear of a man that was the heart beat behind a successful rival.

The hatred was fuelled by the perception of Terry as "*Mr.Chelsea*", like so many other Chelsea fans this is what made him such an inspirational figure. The roar of the Chelsea Lion, the blue blood, the passion, and the relentless journey to dedicate himself to Chelsea to deliver the success that he and every Chelsea fan craved. Week in week out he would put his body in harm's way for the cause of the club, leading by example and inspiring the team towards untold success'.

I like many others will never forget his penalty miss in Moscow, yet his courage and commitment thereafter will always outshine that moment. What I admired about Terry was his ability to go again and deliver even more success to the Chelsea fans. His spirit has undoubtedly lived on through the club and continues to inspire a continuous desire to win and achieve success on every level. Aside from getting hugely familiar with Terry's trophy lifts across his trophy laden career, John's headed goal against Barcelona in the Champions League, that allowed us to proceed to the next round is an outstanding moment at Stamford Bridge I will never forget.

DIDIER DROGBA
FROM: 2004-2012, 2014-2015

Drogba arrived at Stamford Bridge in 2003/2004 season from French Side Marseille. The legacy he would leave behind represents fiction at its finest. Far from a fan favourite when he first joined Chelsea, as frequent diving, injuries, a far from prolific first two seasons and continuous talk of leaving Chelsea were frowned upon. Didier Drogba was a man that often had a point to prove and he would prove it with incredible impact. He was always the man to step up to the biggest occasion, reflected in his incredible cup finals record scoring nine in nine finals. Drogba would be the unstoppable force in so many games against the top sides in the league, domestic and European cup competitions. An absolute menace to opposing defences and unmeasurable inspiration to his teammates. For Chelsea fans he will always be remembered for a particular penalty in Munich, but it his journey to that moment that really highlights the importance and legendary status at the Club.

I remember being at the Champions League Final in Moscow 2008 with my Dad and saying to him as Didier Drogba left the pitch after being sent off in extra time *"he will leave in the summer"*. We would famously go on to lose that final to Manchester United. Nevertheless, he would stay at the club and rewrite a completely different final chapter in the Chelsea history books. The following season, further drama surrounding him at the end of a crushing last minute 1-1 draw with Barcelona in the Champions League Semi final was followed by a great headed finish in the FA Cup final win against Everton. The next season, he would be the goal machine behind winning the Premier League and FA Cup double.

In 2012, four years after the events in Moscow, we would watch Drogba provide a driving force on route to the Champions League final in Munich. A thunderous Didier Drogba header would drag Chelsea back into a Champions League final we had barely featured. Giving away a penalty to Bayern Munich in extra time only to see it saved by Petr Cech. It was written that in that moment, the Didier Drogba rollercoaster would reach its climax. A two step run up, a deceiving glance at the opposite corner sending the keeper the other way, and the ball rolling into the bottom left hand corner. The loudest roar ever from 10,000 Chelsea fans, in a stadium packed with Bayern Munich fans in their city, their stadium. Didier Drogba had delivered the first European Cup in Chelsea's history.

Like all kings their reign is often turbulent, but unlike so many Drogba's would end like the greatest blockbuster movie of all time. **Drogba Legend.**

FRANK LAMPARD
FROM: 2001-2014

On a personal level Frank Lampard was the image of Chelsea. A man who was an inspiration both on and off the pitch. He played for the shirt, the club and it was the opportunity to watch him play that would give me extra incentive to make the drive from Bournemouth to Stamford Bridge multiple times a week. Unlike any other player, he was the man for every occasion which is reflected in the number of goals and assists he has scored in all competitions. If there was ever a player I would encourage any aspiring footballer to emulate, it is Frank Lampard. An incredible talent, with the drive and desire to achieve even more and give every ounce even in the darkest moments.

There are countless defining memories, that underpin my view of Lampard as the greatest of all time. Moments, which in the histories books might just look like a last minute winner against lower competition, but it is those moments that elevate the iconic memories that we all remember to even greater heights. The two goals he scored at Bolton in 2004 to clinch the clubs first Premier League title in fifty years, assisting the goal that won the FA Cup against Manchester United in 2007, an unforgettable penalty against Liverpool in the 2008 Champions League Semi Final following the death of his mother, scoring in the final in Moscow, scoring the winner in the FA Cup Final against Everton, Captaining the side that won the Champions League in 2012 and the UEFA Cup in 2013.

Frank Lampard might not be the king, but he is the super hero of Chelsea FC: "Super Frankie Lampard".

Super, super Frank!
super, super Frank!
super, super Frank!

SUPER FRANKIE LAMPARD!!!

GREATEST CUP GAMES

LIVE FROM STAMFORD BRIDGE SINCE '93

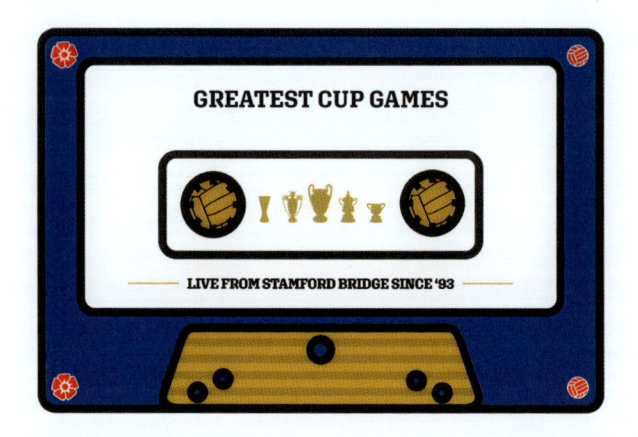

The shift in dynamic from a league to a cup game may not seem much on paper, but when it comes to the contest it's a whole different experience. Teams often take a "nothing to lose" attitude and go for broke to avoid an unwanted replay and fixture pile up. The prospect of getting closer to a potential final and silverware in the trophy cabinet is always a lure that creates different dynamics both on an off the pitch. Goals being scored in volumes that would be unheard of in league matches, different players getting the opportunity to imprint their mark on the team and away goals in Europe creating some of the most tense atmospheres I have ever seen at Stamford Bridge. Cup games are an electrifying experience at the Bridge. My first came in 1995 against Brugges in the European Cup Winners Cup. I had never experienced anything like it. Ever since that night there has always been a real magic about European football under the stars, a whole different feeling compared to a 3pm Saturday kick-off. Huge levels of anticipation and often a welcome reprieve from an ongoing battle in the league.

Since 1993 Stamford Bridge has played host to so many incredible cup occasions domestically and in Europe. Many have lead to massive Chelsea success, whilst others have left the most unpleasant feeling in the pit of your stomach. All the same it's the prospect of enjoying even greater highs and enjoying more success that inspires me to take the 6 hour round trip from Bournemouth to Stamford Bridge on weeknights and weekends. Here are my favourite memories from cup games at Stamford Bridge over the past twenty five years.

CHELSEA 5
WATFORD 0

Sturridge (5), Eustace (og, 15), Malouda (22), Lampard (64), Sturridge (68)
Sunday 3rd January 2010

For many this game would be remembered as a straight forward FA Cup win against a Watford side who were in the lower divisions at the time. The fans inside the Bridge seemed to be more excited that Manchester United had lost 1-0 at home against lower league Leeds United, knocking them out of the competition. I remember it well for a number of reasons. My Dad and I were sitting in the Matthew Harding lower, which represented a change from our seats in the lower West Stand. A new seat, new perspective but a familiar outcome as Chelsea were 3-0 up after twenty minutes and scored 2 goals after half time to secure a convincing 5-0 victory.

It was the events that followed that made this FA Cup tie such a significant one. My Dad and I would go and visit my Grandad in the hospital after the game. He clearly wasn't well, but it was nice to bring him the good news that Chelsea had won 5-0. Despite his condition, his sense of humour hadn't left him and he still made a joke about me and my Dad looking like a couple of gangsters in matching black jackets. It was to be the last time I would see him, and it meant something that we could bring him positive news about the team that we loved. I will never forget that day.

GOAL ALERT!
Zola v Norwich (Wednesday 16th January 2002)

In 2002 many Chelsea fans may have accepted that Gianfranco Zola's magical capabilities were starting to fade. It had been six years since he arrived at the Bridge to conjure up countless moments of genius on the sacred turf and it was expected that his playing days for Chelsea would soon come to an end. On that very special evening Zola had one more trick and like all great magicians he had saved the best for last. Leading 2-0 against Norwich in the FA Cup third tie, Graeme Le Seux would swing a corner into the box. Meeting it in mid-air Zola would allow the ball to pass his left foot and clip the heel off his right foot that was slightly behind him. The ball would find its way into the Norwich net and make it 3-0. A beautiful goal. This goal was extra special for me as it was one I would share with my Grandad from our seats in the shed end. Like all Chelsea fans we were both huge admirers of Zola and hadn't expected to see him deliver one of his most iconic moments on that cold January evening. It was the last match I attended with my Grandad and a moment perfectly suited to the occasion.

CHELSEA 3
TOTTENHAM 3
Lampard (22,71), Kalou (86)
Sunday 10th March 2007

There have been plenty of victories over Tottenham and various other big clubs but the 3-3 in the Quarter Final of the FA Cup in 2007, was truly something special. Chelsea were simply not at the races in the first half. Tottenham took the lead inside five minutes through Berbatov. A brief revival thanks to Lampard's goal just after 20 minutes was short lived as we went in 3-1 down at half time.

The feeling in the stadium at the time was one of disbelief. This was an era in which we just didn't lose to Tottenham, home or away. This isn't to say defeat to Spurs is acceptable today, but in this moment it felt like our hoodoo over them was going to be dispelled. New emotions, new fears and thoughts of the bragging rights repercussions had reached unprecedented heights during that half time interval. It was difficult to see anything but further Spurs dominance and we stood to be on the receiving end of a humiliating defeat to one of our closest rivals. The mind was in *"prepare for the consequences"* mode.

It was incredible comeback in the second half that lead to us grasping a replay at White Heart Lane. Lampard scored in the 71st minute and Kalou was the saviour on 86 to give us the famous draw. The feeling of coming back from certain defeat against Spurs is what makes this game such a significant one. It was a massive show of character and a day you came away from the ground not just relieved but immensely proud of your team. The positive vibes about this game were cemented when we won the return leg at Spurs 2-1 and went on to win the first FA Cup at the new Wembley.

CHELSEA 3
ARSENAL 1
Hughes (10), Di Matteo (51), Petrescu (53)
Wednesday 18th February 1998

In the mid-90's and 2000's we just didn't beat Arsenal. They would always find a way to win or get a draw. As a fan at the Bridge, you always felt a degree of inevitability when a lead was lost to our London rivals. There was a genuine togetherness in that emotion throughout the crowd, an unease and uncertainty. Such was the talent they had at their disposal, through that period including the likes of Henry, Wiltord, Overmars, Bergkamp, Pires and Anelka you knew they could change a game in a second.

Trailing 2-1 from the first leg at Highbury, there was a mountain to climb to turn the tie on its head. To add to the drama Ruud Gullit, the Manager who had lead our FA Cup triumph the season before had been sacked just days before. Gianluca Vialli had been given the role of Player Manager and would represent the beginning of a long line of successful Italian Managers at Chelsea. The odds were firmly against us, but as we would come to discover in many seasons thereafter, Chelsea were at their most dangerous when the media had written us off.

As a spectacle it was a truly scintillating night of football at Stamford Bridge. The big game players such as Zola, Hughes, Di-matteo, Petrescu and Vialli were all inspired to give the fans something to cheer about after days of uncertainty surrounding the club. A superb swivel and shot from the edge of the box from Mark Hughes would give us the lead on the night and level the scores at 2-2. The second half would see Roberto Di Matteo deliver a rocket launcher strike not dissimilar to his goal in the FA Cup Final in 1997 to take it to 2-0 and 3-2 on Aggregate. *"Super"* Dan Petrescu would show quick feet in the box to pass two Arsenal players and strike a third into the net. The Bridge was rocking, as we began to believe we would be returning to Wembley for a second successive season.

Despite a late consolation goal from a Bergkamp penalty we would see the game through and clinch our place in the League Cup Final. *"Que*

Sera, Sera, We are going to Wembley"* was the roar from the Chelsea fans. The song seemed fitting on a night where uncertainty surrounded the Club as *"whatever we will be"* we were going to Wembley and as a Chelsea fan that meant everything.

GOAL ALERT!
Gudjohnsen vs. Leeds (Tuesday 28th January 2003)

15 at the time and just over 15 years ago, one of my Chelsea hero's scored an incredible goal against Leeds United. Known for his excellent link-up play, intelligent thinking and deft touch in front of goal Eidur Gudjohnsen popped up with an incredible overhead kick to make it 1-1 during this mid-week clash with fierce rivals Leeds United. The game would end 3-2 to Chelsea and would prove to be a hugely valuable 3 points in pushing us towards a Champions League spot. It was a spectacular goal: A pre-world class Frank Lampard dug out an inviting cross into the box which seemed as if it would go to waste and defy everyone in the box. Eidur Gudjohnsen had other ideas. In a blink of an eye, he was propelled into a fantastic scissor kick, latching onto the fast paced cross and smashing the ball past Paul Robinson into the Leeds goal. An incredible goal.One of the best ever scored in Premier League history and one of the best I have ever seen live.

Younger football fans reading this will be familiar with Cristiano Ronaldo's overhead kick for Real Madrid in the Champions League semi final against Juventus. This beauty from Eidur Gudjohnsen is very similar. But if the Goal wasn't good enough it was followed up by what would become (for me at least) one of the classiest football celebrations ever. Gudjohnsen wheeled away towards the Leeds fans in the corner, pointing at his eye while looking at the Chelsea fans as if to say *"watch this"* and having managed to momentarily get his team mates off his back, he gave the *"Icelandic bow"*. A simple joining of the hands and spreading them in an outward motion. An epic Chelsea goal celebration suited to the class act that was the *"Ice Man"*. That celebration would go on to cement my perception of Gudjohnsen as one of my heroes, but would also become the signature celebration I would steal and be known for on the playground, my school and weekend teams. I think most people thought I was a cocky for doing it, but who cares I loved it.

CHELSEA 2
BRUGES 0
Stein (16), Furlong (38)
Tuesday 14th March 1995

In 1995 I had my first taste of European Football, a big quarter final against Bruges in the Cup Winners Cup. We had lost the first leg 1-0 and needed to win by two clear goals to qualify. In the mid-1990's this was a massive game, the Chelsea faithful were yet to embrace the massive Champions League ties that would follow in years to come. Attending a game under a floodlight Stamford Bridge was a whole new experience compared to a daytime match. Sitting in the east stand lower, Stamford Bridge felt different, the crowds were more vocal and there was greater sense of aggression in the air. As a seven year old it was an intimidating place to be. The fans had come to let off steam from their work day and needed a reason to get up the next morning. Chelsea had to win.

It proved to be an incredible night to be at the Bridge. Wearing our worst ever away kit (orange and grey), we took an early lead through Mark Stein. Through the thick of punching fists and men jumping around I remember seeing him come over to the corner at our end and perform his trademark crossed arms celebration. It was one of those moments as a kid, when you would say to yourself I want to be that guy when I'm older. To have the fans going that crazy and being able to casually celebrate in front of them like a superhero. To be that close to one of the players had a real really surreal feel about it, they were superhuman, untouchable. As you get older it's funny how whilst you still feel in awe of the players, your appreciate they are humans who have worked extremely hard to be successful footballers. It's a good lesson to kids that by being committed to something you can achieve your goals. It was an important moment for me in shaping my dream of being a football player when I was older.

We would go on to get the second goal later in the first half through Paul Furlong and manage to keep them from scoring to qualify for the semi-finals of the Cup Winners Cup. It was a massive night at the Bridge and one that will stay with me for many reasons.

CHELSEA 3
BARCELONA 1
Zola (30), Flo (34.38)
Wednesday 5th April 2000

Back in 2000 reaching the Quarter Finals of the Champions League was beyond unfamiliar territory for Chelsea. Aside from lifting the Cup Winners cup trophy in 1998, Chelsea had no where near the same profile in Europe as they do today. The epic 3-1 victory over Barcelona is a match where Chelsea stamped there name into the elite European competition and would provide the pathway to the success that would follow. For those who remember, it was an incredible night at Stamford Bridge. Back then playing against the Spanish giants was an achievement in itself and a draw would have been a great result.

Zola, La-La-La-La Zola!

Eden, Eden, Eden, Eden, Eden, Eden Hazard!

Chelsea fans were in for a treat. A sublime free-kick from Gianfranco Zola on 30 minutes sent the stands into raptures and the goal spree that followed left everyone wondering whether Stamford Bridge was able to withstand such scenes of celebration and excitement.

The display was like no other before it, and only one match a few years later against the same opponents could exceed the scenes of jubilation in such a short period of time. This was the stuff of legend, that would live long in the memory of Chelsea fans in attendance and watching at home on the TV. Barcelona would get a crucial away in the second half to end the first leg 3-1, but that didn't stop the Chelsea's fans celebrating long into the night.

CHELSEA 4
BAYERN MUNICH 2
Lucio (5 og), Lampard (59, 70), Drogba (81)
Wednesday 6th April 2005

The 2004/5 season was when Frank Lampard set the domestic and European stage on fire. The epic Wednesday night in April was a stage where the Lampard beacon would shine its brightest. In terms of the teams overall display it was a momentous one, that is only overshadowed by the events that had occurred the month before against Barcelona. Chelsea were an absolute force and were taking Europe and the Premier League by storm.

An early lead was achieved from a Bayern Munich own goal following a wayward effort from Joe Cole. The second half would prove to be a goal bonanza, with Bayern Munich levelling on 53 when Chelsea should have been out of sight. Lampard would respond 6 minutes later with a great left footed finish from the edge of the box. However, it was on 70 minutes that Lampard would leave 40,000 jaws firmly on the floor. An awkward ball would arrive chest high, and after a single touch Lampard spun and struck an incredible volley past the helpless Kahn in goal. It's one of the greatest goals ever at Stamford Bridge and possibly the best of the 211 that Lampard has scored during his incredible career. Drogba would go on to add a 4th 10 minutes from time. Michael Ballack (a Bayern Munich player at the time) would place a minor question mark over our eventual qualification with a late goal from the spot. Another special night and another Super Frank Masterclass.

GOAL ALERT!

Drogba vs. Barcelona (Wednesday 18th October 2006)

The ball arrives at your feet, back to goal on the edge of the box and Carlos Puyol one of the most coveted defenders in world football is breathing down your neck. What do you? The sensible thing would be to hold it up and lay it back to one of the oncoming midfielders. That would get you a good pat on the back from the boss. However, if you are Didier Drogba instead you give the Spanish superstar a sight of the ball and entice him into applying some pressure. In a blink of an eye you flick the ball away from him, still back to goal, create the tightest of angles and bang. Plant the ball into the right hand side of the net. A truly incredible goal, against one of the greatest defenders and greatest teams of all time. Chelsea would go on to win the game 1-0 thanks to that incredible strike.

CHELSEA 4
LIVERPOOL 4

Drogba (52), Alex (57), Lampard (76, 89)
Tuesday 14th April 2009

When it comes to sheer entertainment it's difficult to top the clash with Liverpool in the Quarter Final of the Champions League in 2009. We went into the match with a strong 3-1 lead from the first leg at Anfield. Liverpool obviously had other ideas, racing into a 2-0 lead in the first half and leaving us with merely a superior away goal advantage putting us through. It was the second half that the roof almost went into orbit following a blitz of goals. Drogba scoring from the tightest of angles, Alex's thunderous free kick and a Frank Lampard trademark goal turned the game on its head and seemingly put the tie beyond doubt. Liverpool had different ideas (again), with 2 goals in 2 minutes making them need only 1 goal to qualify themselves on goal difference. Up stood Frank Lampard once again and crashed home a stunning effort via both posts from the edge of the box. 4-4 game over. A night of true Champions League drama, a rollercoaster of emotions and the result we needed to get through to the next round. An epic Champions League night at the Bridge and it was only a draw.

CHELSEA 4
NAPOLI 1

Drogba (29), Terry (48), Lampard (75 pen), Ivanovic (105)
Wednesday 14th March 2012

On reflection many Chelsea fans would consider the 4-1 victory over Napoli as the night Chelsea's name was engraved on the European Cup for the first time. From that evening it was written in the stars. For those, who remember the club was in absolute meltdown at the time.

Chelsea were lucky to lose the away leg in Naples 3-1, Andre Villas Boas had been sacked as boss, Champions League qualification for the next season via the league was unlikely, we had barely got passed Birmingham to get through to the next round of the FA Cup. On top of that this was a Chelsea team, that despite sporting some of its greatest players of all time (Drogba, Lampard, Terry and Cech) was in its twilight years. Incredible experience, but not quite the physical capabilities they had eight years previously. If ever there was a Chelsea team that would never give in this was it. Despite multiple failings in Champions League competition in 2005 (Liverpool), 2006 (Liverpool) 2008 (Man Utd Final), 2009 (Barcelona semi). This team of Chelsea "has-beens" would go on to produce one of the greatest come backs and occasions at Stamford Bridge in recent memory.

A first half goal from King Didier, followed by our clinical captain Terry in the second half appeared to turn the tie in our favour. However, Napoli struck back to make it 2-1, which would put them through on away goals. Thankfully Lampard would deliver from the spot once again to to take the tie into extra time. The three musketeers and ever reliable spine to Chelsea's success' in the previous decade had returned to save the day once again. With the tie seemingly heading to penalties Ivanovic would fire home from the edge of the box to seal an incredible victory.

The scenes at the Bridge were unforgettable. Just the small matter of beating Benfica, Barcelona and Bayern Munich would stand in the path of glory. Easy.

GOAL ALERT!
Zola vs. West Ham (Saturday 21st December 1996)

Back in 1996 the rivalry with West Ham at least from a Chelsea perspective was greater than it was today. There were three consecutive seasons (1994, 1995 and 1996) where we would be fighting them for league position supremacy, albeit around mid-table. Gianfranco Zola's scintillating run and strike proved to be the perfect Christmas gift and a indication to our London rivals that we were on the ascendancy. With the daunting figure of Julian Dicks breathing down his neck and the intention of stop him at any cost, Zola the Italian magician was able to wriggle away from his impending grasp, look him in the eyes with the ball at his feet, magically dummy the claret and blue giant and smash the ball into the bottom left corner. Julian Dicks was never the same scary figure since and West Ham would soon be left in behind in a cloud of blue smoke. A beautiful goal and an unforgettable memory from that period.

CHELSEA 3
LIVERPOOL 2
Drogba (33), Lampard (98), Drogba (105)
Wednesday 30th April 2008

Final and Frank Lampard are the key ingredient behind this stormy semi-final Champions League tie. It is quite possibly the most emotionally charged game of football that I have ever been to. Frank Lampard's mother had passed away the week before and a Champions League Final was at stake. As a fan it was incredible to see Frank Lampard on the pitch, let alone see him stepping up to fulfil the pivotal role he would play in our qualification. No doubt using the biggest stage in European football to help handle the emotions he must have been going through.

Frank would go on to produce one of the most iconic moments of his Chelsea career and further cement his place as an all time Chelsea hero. The standard 90 minutes would end 1-1 following a first half goal from Drogba, and an equaliser from Torres in the second half. It was in Extra time that Lampard would show incredible courage to step up and place the ball on the spot. Fans around us found it hard to watch, the tension, the anxiety that was in the ground at that moment. Frank swept the ball home, ran towards the corner flag and fell to his knees, kissing the Captains armband, with tears in his eyes. The Bridge was absolutely rocking with a multitude of emotions. Happiness at re-taking the lead, but also relief and an outpouring of respect for Frank Lampard for stepping up in the biggest moment of the clubs history (at the time) and possibly the toughest moment of his. We would go on to win 3-2 and reach our first Champions league final, following a goal from Didier Drogba and a nerve jangling consolation from Babel for Liverpool.

Moscow awaits.

CHELSEA 4
BARCELONA 2

Gudjohnsen (8), Lampard (17), Duff (19), Terry (76)
Tuesday 8th March 2005

This is the greatest night of Champions League football ever to grace the green grass of Stamford Bridge. Despite only being a first round tie, it is the sheer quality and atmosphere that was present on the night that makes this game so special. Combined with the fact that Chelsea hadn't quite established themselves amongst the European elite, gave this game extra significance.

Following a 2-1 defeat to Barcelona at the Nou Camp in the first leg it was up to Chelsea to respond to keep any Champions League hopes alive. The first 20 minutes was more than a response, it was a volcanic eruption. Gudjonhsen, Lampard and Duff would send Stamford Bridge into absolute delirium as we stormed into a 3-0 lead inside 19 minutes. Remember this wasn't just any old team, this was the Spanish giants featuring Ronaldinho, Xavi, Inesta, Puyol, Xavi and Eto'o. Of course it was and it was the role that one particular Barcelona player would perform that truly made the evening even more special. The world's best player at the time Ronaldinho would first score a straight forward penalty, but it was the goal that followed that left the Stamford Bridge faithful speechless. An audacious effort with the outside of the foot eluded everyone inside the stadium and nestled its place in Cech's goal. An incredible goal, fitting for such a spectacular night of European football.Barcelona were now back in the driving seat after being dead and buried after our rampaging opening 20 minutes. The

Spanish giants appeared to have a greater foothold in the game now and we looked lacking of ideas in search of the goal we needed to clinch the tie. "*Captain. Leader. Legend.*" John Terry would put us through with an iconic header from a set play and classic intervention from Carvalho. The night and tie was ours. From that moment Chelsea were part of the big time.

GOAL ALERT!
Drogba vs. Liverpool (Sunday 17th September 2006)

It in the height of the September sun a scintillating strike from Didier Drogba would prove to be the difference between us and our close rivals Liverpool. Jamie Carragher was clawing at the Ivorian's back as he took the the ball high on his chest on the edge of Liverpool box. For most of the fans in the bridge it would look like an awkward one, instead of falling straight to his feet it would pop up and slightly away giving Didier a lot of work to do to face the goal. The goal machine had different ideas, using the apparent lack of an opportunity to peel away from Carragher, plant one foot in the ground, allow the ball to bounce and swivel while striking the ball with incredible vigour with his left foot on the half volley. No one had been expecting the shot to come at that moment, and Pepe Reina and the Liverpool defence could only watch as the ball flew into the back of the net. A moment of pure class and fitting way to separate two teams vying for the top position. Stamford Bridge went wild, Chelsea won 1-0, three valuable points.

We'll keep the blue flag flying high, we'll keep the blue flag flying high, from Stamford Bridge to Wembley, we'll keep the blue flag flying high!

1997

2000   2007

2009   2010   2012   2018

1998   2004   2007   2015

www.throwbackblues.com

TOP 10 CHELSEA MANAGERS

LIVE FROM STAMFORD BRIDGE SINCE '93

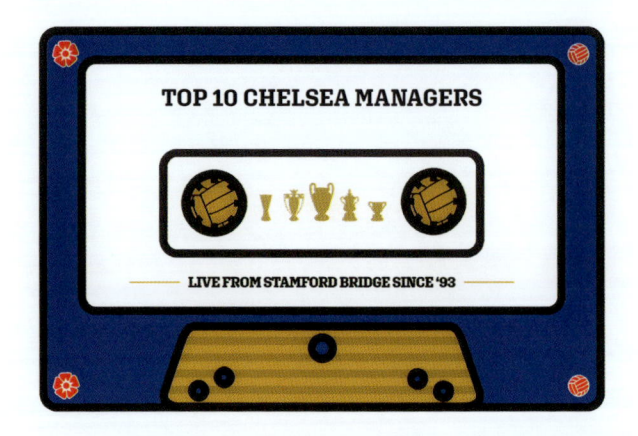

Such is the rotational nature of the Stamford Bridge Managerial entry and exit door, I have the pleasure of being able to deliver my verdict on the greatest Managers to ply their technical craft to a star studded team sheet. Across those twenty five years, we really have seen some of the finest tacticians and masterminds of world football, with almost all of them providing the Stamford Bridge faithful with silverware.

From Glenn Hoddle, right through Vialli, Scolari, Avram Grant, Mourihno, Conte and Ancelotti there has been incredible names standing in the home dugout during my visits to Stamford Bridge since 1993. Each providing magical moments in an attempt to entertain and deliver the success that the Stamford Bridge faithful continues to demand today.

When putting together my shortlist of Greatest Chelsea Managers, careful consideration for the era and the importance of their tenure at the helm of our beloved club is of paramount importance.

RAFA BENITEZ
FROM: 2012-2013

Having read those two words I can imagine many Chelsea fans may be tempted to close this book and toss it in the fire. Rafa Benitez's affiliation with Liverpool made him a hugely unpopular figure during his time at Stamford Bridge. We even had a song for him that was an obvious sign of our displeasure at his appointment. What's more his appointment came following the dismissal of Chelsea legend Roberto Di Matteo who had guided the club to the FA and European Cup double the season before. Impossible shoes to fill. However, the hostility surrounding him and the success he did manage to achieve in that situation makes him marginally ahead of Avram Grant in my perception of greatest Chelsea Managers.

It could have been so different if Grant had won the League Cup against Spurs in 2008, Terry had scored the penalty in the Champions League Final in Moscow and we had been able to claim Premier League title. However, without wishing to devalue Avram Grant's impact during his time in charge, as a fan it felt that it was the players rather than the Manager that was driving that team towards the brink of massive success. The likes of Lampard, Terry and Drogba maintained the Mourinho ethos as they aimed to bring home silverware to the Chelsea fans. Without Didier Drogba to spearhead the Chelsea frontline In 2013 there was a lot more riding on Rafa Benitez's managerial input to get the most from an under performing Fernando Torres, guide us to UEFA Cup glory and seel Champions League qualification by finishing 3rd. Rafa Benitez was the man who brought us our first ever UEFA Cup, enabling us to become only the 4th club in history to win all three European trophies (Cup Winners Cup, European Cup and UEFA Cup). In addition we would be the first club ever to hold both the European Cup and the UEFA Cup at the same time. Rafa may not care about Chelsea and we might not care about him, but as long as we care about Chelsea we can never forget the success he brought to our club.

CLAUDIO RANIERI
FROM: 2001-2004

Despite failing to deliver any silverware to the Chelsea trophy cabinet, Claudio Raneiri's impact at the club should never be understated. He was the man who built a large part of the team that Jose Mourinho would lead to numerous triumphs. Players such as Frank Lampard, Claude Makelele, William Gallas, Joe Cole, Wayne Bridge and Damien Duff were all purchased under Raneiri's watch and he also played a significant role in Didier Drogba and Arjen Robben's arrival at the club the season following his departure.

Despite eventual acceptance there was a feeling of sadness from the Stamford Bridge faithful as it seemed inevitable he would leave the club at the end of the 2003 season. Despite leading us to an FA Cup Final in 2002, The Semi Final of the Champions League in 2003 and four successive years of improved league points his time was up as Abramovich demanded silverware to show for his significant investment in the club. My fondest memory of Ranieri as Chelsea Manager was the smile and happiness on his face following our victory over Arsenal at Highbury in the Champions League Quarter-final in 2003. However, I think his downfall came in the following round as a heavy 3-1 away to in Monaco would lead to eventual elimination at Stamford Bridge. It was that tie in which he would always be remembered as the *"The Tinkerman"* for making changes to the team where perhaps they weren't needed. Simply on a human level the departure of Ranieri was a tough one to take, he was loved by the fans and for all of us it filled us all with happiness to see him finally achieve the success he deserved in 2016 when he guided Leicester to Premier League glory.

GLENN HODDLE
FROM: 1993-1996

As the Manager of Chelsea FC to be in the dugout when I first took my own seat at Stamford Bridge in 1993, I will always hold Glenn Hoddle in highest regard. At the time I wasn't aware of his ties with Tottenham, so you can imagine I saw him as a Chelsea man especially as he was a member of the playing side as well as being Manager. Hoddle guided the club to an FA Cup Final in 1994, which we lost 4-0 to Manchester United. Despite the heavy defeat reaching an FA Cup Final was massive achievement for the club at that time. I didn't attend the game, but it was the first time I had felt the excitement, anxiety and anticipation surrounding the FA Cup build up. It was an incredible experience to be a part of at seven years old, a real eye opener to the importance of Football nationwide. Despite defeat, we would still enter the European Cup Winners Cup as Manchester and would enter the European Cup following their Premier League success. It was during the season of 1994/1995 I was able to enjoy my first taste of European Football and watch Chelsea reach the semi-final of a European competition was really something special. The value of Glenn Hoddle's time as Chelsea Manager was established further by being able to attract big names to the club, the arrival of Ruud Gullitt would lead to a wave of quality overseas players and subsequent success in the seasons after.

GUUS HIDDINK
2009

Despite overseeing a mere four month management spell at Stamford Bridge his impact on the team was profound. In the wake of Scolari's departure following a downturn in performances Hiddink was able to regalvanise the team and bring success at the end of the season. Under different circumstances his legacy may have been even more significant.

During his short spell Hiddink only lost on a single occasion, 1-0 away to Spurs which proved to derail any glimmer of hope of mounting a challenge for the League title. Yet it was the Champions League Semi Final that Chelsea fans will feel Hiddink's story was cut short. Following a 0-0 draw in the Nou Camp, Chelsea held a commanding 1-0 lead over Barcelona at Stamford Bridge only for Andreas Iniesta to famously equalize and put Barcelona through. There was no issues over the goal from Chelsea fans but the referee's display was surrounded by controversy, failing to award any of the six penalty claims during the ninety minutes. I remember the sixth one well from where we were sitting as Michael Ballack screamed at the referee following his inability to take action against the Barcelona defender raising his arms to block his shot. Despite this disappointment Hiddink would pick the players up again and guide them to a 2-1 win the FA Cup Final against Everton, the least he deserved for what appeared to be an untenable position upon his arrival.

*Que sera, sera,
whatever we will be, will be,
we are going to Wembley,
que sera, sera!*

*Que sera, sera,
whatever we will be, will be,
we are going to Wembley,
que sera, sera!*

Hearing this being sung at full voice by 20,000 Chelsea fans at Highbury, after Mark Hughes had all but sealed our place in the 1997 FA Cup Final with a goal to put us 3-0 up against Wimbledon. My first trip to Wembley was on the horizon!

1997

GIANLUCA VIALLI
FROM: 1998-2000

As player/Manager for Chelsea following his rapid appointment to succeed the sacked Ruud Gullit in February 1998, Gianluca Vialli would guide the team to League Cup and European Cup Winners Cup success in that season. An emphatic victory against Arsenal just days after Vialli's appointment would ensure Chelsea's passage to Wembley and an eventual 2-0 victory over Middlesbrough in the final. A stunning individual effort from Zola 30 seconds after coming on would ensure European silverware would also arrive at Stamford Bridge that season. Vialli guided Chelsea to their only Super Cup success with a 1-0 win over Real Madrid in Monaco thanks to a late Poyet goal and add further silverware in 2000 by winning the last FA Cup Final at the old Wembley with a 1-0 win over Aston Villa. Roberto Di Matteo on target again to clinch victory for the Blues. Vialli undoubtedly delivered silverware and continued the quality style of football that the fans demanded, but I can't help but feel slightly bitter about some of of his time as Manager. The sacking of Ruud Gullit, was my first experience of controversy surrounding a Manager leaving the club. Today the media would hype it up a managers departure for so long via the internet and social media, it seemed a case of when and not if. I remember my dad showing me the back page of the paper confirming Ruud Gullit's departure and I just felt a bit lost about it all. To have everything I loved about the club suddenly shattered, it was a range of new negative emotions I hadn't really experienced before when it came to Football. I was probably still living off the success of the FA Cup victory the year before and it was a real eye opener to the cut and thrust nature of the real world let alone football. Of course today as Chelsea fans we have become accustomed to regular change in Managerial roles, taking it in our stride but back then it really did impact me and has stayed with me as a significant memory to this day.

RUUD GULLIT
FROM: 1996-1998

Chelsea's first piece of silverware for twenty six years will be the long lasting memory fans will have of Ruud Gullit's management of Chelsea. Promoted from player to player/manager in the Summer of 1996 following the departure of Glenn Hoddle for England, Gullit would bring a world of change to Chelsea Football Club. A change that would shape the clubs future towards even greater success. Such was Gullit's global status he was able to attract stars such as Gianfranco Zola, Gianluca Vialli, Frank Leboeuf, Dan Petrescu and Roberto Di Matteo. With it came a new breed of football at Stamford Bridge, that would be known as *"sexy football"* a type of football the fans at Stamford Bridge had never seen. The 1996/1997 season Stamford Bridge was quite simply an incredible place to be. Other than against the top clubs, you went with the expectation of goals, entertainment and victory. You also couldn't wait to see what new celebrations the Chelsea players would bring following each goal scored. It was the first time I had felt an atmosphere of belief and anticipation within the ground, Stamford Bridge was a genuine theatre of entertainment. The climax of that season would be lifting the FA Cup at Wembley, my first taste of Chelsea successfully winning silverware felt incredible given that the club had waited so long for the day to arrive. *"The blue tomorrow"* had officially arrived.

ANTONIO CONTE
FROM: 2016-2018

Belief was at a low point at Stamford Bridge when Antonio Conte joined Chelsea in the summer of 2016. His arrival came off the back of a disastrous 10th place finish in 2016, following winning the Premier League in the 2014/15 season. As a result expectations from fans were no longer at the level they were used to as the winning aura surrounding the club seemed to be fading. Getting back in the Champions League was probably the maximum we could hope to achieve, with reclaiming the title well off the agenda considering the capitulation the season before. Antonio's tenure at the club, particularly during his first season is probably one of the most enjoyable I can remember as a Chelsea fan inside Stamford Bridge.

His passion and commitment on the sidelines is exactly what we needed from the manager at that time. Even in the wake of two resounding defeats to Arsenal and Liverpool early in the season, it was Conte's drive that really struck a chord with the Stamford Bridge faithful. We may have lost players such as Drogba, Lampard, and Cech who carried the Chelsea flag with such vigour, but in their place came Conte who was a man who would resuscitate the Chelsea faithful and rekindle the winning mentality that everyone thought had been lost. Antonio's elaborate goal celebrations, rubbing it in Mourinho's face after beat Manchester United 4-0, and always addressing the crowd with such jubilation following a victory filled Chelsea fans with an incredible sense of belief. Singing Antonio's name from the West Stand Lower week in week out was a sign of how much the Chelsea fans appreciated what he had done to get the club and the players back on their feet.

Against the odds he would mastermind the change to a 3-5-2 formation and guide us with sheer grit and determination to Premier League glory. Claiming the trophy ahead of close rivals Spurs and some of the most incredible scenes of celebration at Stamford Bridge, are the true representation of his Chelsea Legacy. It was disappointing we were unable to add the FA Cup that season following defeat to Arsenal in the final. Unfortunately his second season in charge was a turbulent one, with transfer and club control issues continuously surrounding the events on the pitch. Even in the early stages of the season it appeared to be the beginning of the end for Antonio Conte at Chelsea. However, despite only finishing fifth in the league, Conte did lead the club to success in the FA Cup final masterminding a 1-0 victory against Jose Mourinho's Manchester United. With two trophies to his name and massive adoration from the Stamford Bridge faithful, Conte will always be one of Chelsea's finest. *"Grazie, Antonio!"*

ROBERTO DI MATTEO
2012

As far as tactical knowledge and leadership qualities are concerned Roberto Di Matteo is unlikely to be considered Chelsea's best ever. However, his impact in the space of three short months is what makes him undeniably one of Chelsea's greatest. Following a 3-1 defeat away to Napoli in the Champions League, Di Matteo found himself thrown into the Caretaker Manager role to rescue Andre Villas-Boas sinking ship. Given the situation at the club at the time, little did we expect to see him guide the ship to Munich via Wembley and deliver a cup double Chelsea fans could only dream of. The 4-1 victory in the home league against Napoli that took us through, masterminding two incredible ties against Barcelona in the semi final, and beating Spurs 5-1 at Wembley were beyond imagination. He would then somehow finish the job with famous victories over Liverpool in the FA Cup Final, followed by Champions League glory on the greatest night in the clubs history two weeks later in Munich. Di Matteo was at the helm of those achievements and along with his Chelsea playing career will always be considered a Chelsea Legend.

CARLO ANCELOTTI
FROM: 2009-2011

Despite only spending two seasons as Chelsea Manager Ancelotti will also be held in the highest regard following the Premier League and FA Cup double he brought to Stamford Bridge. A massive achievement given the demands of competing in two competitions. What made that achievement even more significant was the response to setbacks during the 2009/10 season. In the aftermath of defeat to Inter Milan in the Champions League few would believe the "ageing" team had the ability to go on and win a trophy let alone a Championship.

A succession of massive wins against Portsmouth, Stoke, Aston Villa and a table turning victory away at Manchester United would pave the way to a Championship title on the last day. The League and cup double would be completed the following week with a 1-0 victory over Portsmouth at Wembley. Carlo Ancelotti had restored belief in a team that were scarred by failures in 2008 and 2009 to deliver unprecedented success in 2010. Carlo's affinity with the players was clear to see in the Chelsea Double Winners Bus Parade by taking the mic on countless occasions to the sing with the players and the fans.

JOSE MOURINHO
FROM: 2004-2007, 2013-2015

Few Chelsea fans can deny that Jose Mourinho is Chelsea's greatest ever Manager. The trophies Chelsea achieved under his management are evidence in itself. However, it wasn't just the trophies that made his importance to the club so significant, it was his winning mentality. A mentality that he enriched into his players, bringing out the best in the likes of Frank Lampard, Didier Drogba, John Terry and Petr Cech. He helped to take those players from great, to world beating superstars. His winning ethos was one that he was able to communicate so effectively to the fans, and considering we hadn't won a League title in fifty years that was some achievement. He enabled us to not only dream of a blue tomorrow, but believe in its inevitability. It was his arrogance and self belief that meant his players and the Chelsea fans believed he could deliver the success the club demanded. The conviction in which he sewed a winning mentality into the clubs DNA has ensured that it still remains their today. There are countless moments during and after matches that Mourinho meticulously instilled this attitude and in return he would claim three Premier Leagues, three league cups and an FA Cup during two spells as Manager.

Personally, the respect and adoration for Mourinho from the Chelsea fans was most visible in the first game of his second spell as Manager. As he appeared from the dugout to take his seat the standing ovation and applause he received was deafening and sent goosebumps down my spine. Many Managers have had their names sung by the Stamford Bridge faithful, but the chant of *"stand up for the special one!"* was a exclusive to one man.

Stand up for the special one!

Stand up for the special one!

2005 2006 2015 2007 2005 2007 2015

www.throwbackblues.com

THE ROLLERCOASTER TO MUNICH

LIVE FROM STAMFORD BRIDGE SINCE '93

Most Chelsea fans will be more than familiar with the epic journey that underpinned the unlikely European Cup in Munich in 2012. For many that journey began well before I was even born, for Chelsea it began back in 1905 when our club was formed. My story of of how we went on to lift the epic trophy will begin seven years before in 2005.

2005 : Losing is Learning

From a Chelsea fan perspective the 2005 Champions League campaign, left a bitter taste at the end of what had been the most incredible domestic season. The jubilance of Premier League and League Cup glory fresh in the mind, would be scuppered by the Garcia "Ghost Goal" for Liverpool in the semi-final that would prevent us from reaching our first ever European Cup Final. I remember feeling a selfish level of disappointment, as the seasons other trophy success' seemed to be overshadowed momentarily by this defeat. As is human nature there is always a hunger for more, casting aside what you have and focusing immediate energy for even more. It's difficult to assess what might have been if that goal hadn't been given, probably a penalty for Liverpool, Chelsea might have won. Today it doesn't matter. In hindsight, would the heroes of 2012 be the Chelsea legends they have become without the bitter taste of failure early in their Chelsea careers? For the players and the fans this was the making of something magical to come, I know that without being knocked to the canvas on this occasion I wouldn't appreciate how incredible Champions League glory is. Either way, getting up off the canvas of defeat would be a recurring theme in the years that followed.

2007 : Deja Vu

If 2005 wasn't our season, then neither was 2007. Again we would fall to Liverpool at the Semi-final stage. I remember the Semi Final at the Bridge well mainly because during my journey from Bournemouth to Stamford Bridge the engine on my Mum's Volkswagen Lupo (that I was driving) would give out and leave me stranded on the motorway for many hours. It turns out cars need oil, and being a laid back "Lazy University student" I chose to ignore the warnings. I wouldn't have blamed my Dad for leaving me there and going to the game on his own, but he made sure I was there and we would go on to win 1-0 thanks to a goal from Joe Cole.

Despite taking a lead to Anfield (which we failed to do in 2005) it still wouldn't be enough as Liverpool took the lead in the first half and the game would go to penalties. We would lose 4-1. I remember sitting in the social lounge at my University accommodation and watching the game. In the immediate aftermath of the penalties Manchester Utd fans jumped on the opportunity to inflict salt to my fresh wounds by asking if I was upset. I ignored the taunts and returned the favour the following night after AC Milan thumped them 3-0 in the San Siro, which meant they wouldn't be in the final either.

2008 : Stranded in Moscow

Undoubtedly there were a couple of uncomfortable Champions League campaigns, but 2008 was probably the toughest of them all. Unlike 2005 and 2007 we would claim victory over Liverpool in the semi-final, burying them as our hoodoo team in European Competition. The nature of the incredible 3-2 victory to get through to the final was one of the most emotionally charged nights I have ever experienced at Stamford Bridge. Frank Lampard's strength to play and step up to take a hugely important penalty despite the recent passing of his mother, was one of the moments that made this night truly special. It's one of many big moments that my Dad and I always refer to when describing why Frank Lampard is the best Chelsea player in history, let alone my lifetime.

Moscow, Russia was now awaiting the arrival of Chelsea, one half of the first ever Champions League Final to be contested by two English Clubs. Manchester United or Chelsea would have their names inscribed on the famous trophy following the evenings events. It's worth noting that this is the first time ever I have relived the experience in detail. It is shrouded by so much negativity that I might make reference to it but not ponder on it for too long. I'm not one to ponder on the negative, unless there is a positive to come of it. My Dad and I did the Moscow final trip in a single day, having been to Moscow a few years previously for a Champions League group game against CSKA Moscow. The day was a bleak one, with heavy storms and grey casting a grim shadow over much of Moscow. Despite being over ten years ago, a day as monumental as this lives with you forever and the atmosphere and importance of being in a European final was evident. The tension was rising throughout the day, with Manchester United as the opponent the plot was thickening even further. I remember we had a short exchange with a couple of United Fans in McDonald's (the food venue of choice it seemed for

English football fans in Moscow), the conversation ended with *"Good luck tonight"* a blatant lie if I had ever heard one. Every Chelsea fan was hungry for victory, especially as we had been pipped by United to the Premier League that season.

It seemed like a long build up to the game, the weather was bleak and the fan park outside of the ground proved to be little more than a prison recreation yard to walk around repetitively before we were allowed to enter the ground. Having found our seats we were welcomed by a large white post on the side of the pitch that was blocking our view, something you expected at White Hart Lane rather a stadium hosting the Champions League Final. Not a positive start to a heart breaking 120+ minutes in the Luzhniki Stadium. Chelsea fans will be well aware of how this one panned out.

Cristiano Ronaldo would give Manchester the lead and Frank Lampard would get us back on level terms before half time. From memory we would go on to dominate much of the game, Didier Drogba crashing the post with a curled effort and Lampard smashing the bar. All what might have been moments, that made you wonder if it was our day. The weather and the contest would worsen as Didier Drogba would receive a red card in extra time following an exchange with Vidic. It was in that moment that I said to my Dad *"He will leave in the summer"*, Didier Drogba was destined to be the Moscow villain in the eyes of Cheslea fans, on a night that didn't seem to be going in our favour.

No further goals meant that penalties would decide the victors. Petr Cech's save from Ronaldo's penalty, created genuine belief the trophy would be coming back to the Bridge. The scenes that would follow would be stamped on the memory of every Chelsea fan who witnessed it. With the chance to win the trophy, John Terry would slip taking his penalty kick and hit the outside of the post. In that moment belief seemed to be sucked from the Chelsea fans and history would forget that it was Nikolas Anelka's penalty miss that would seal defeat.

I remember a lot about the immediate aftermath of the Moscow final. I was waiting outside the toilets for my Dad and remember just crying, overwhelmed by tiredness and the emotion of it all. Thoughts of how much effort my Dad had put in to get us there, this overwhelming sadness that he hadn't got to see them win. I was 20 so I believed there was plenty of opportunities for me, but it wasn't an experience I wanted to have without him. My Dad isn't even that old and is probably cursing me for making it seem like he was on his last legs, but reaching a European Cup final doesn't come around that often. It took Chelsea 103 years to reach their first, we might not be around for the next one!

Nevertheless, it wasn't to be and the nightmare match was followed by a nightmare journey home. Terrible weather was combined with terrible navigation by me and we got lost in search of our bus back to the airport. I fell asleep on the bus and it seemed that those in control at Moscow Airport had done the same as the state of the terminal with Chelsea fans trying to get out of the country really was a catastrophe. The gloom that hung heavily over every Chelsea fan made it feel like there were 2,000 elephants in the room and judging by the fact they didn't seem to have enough space on planes to get everyone home suggested many of those elephants were real. Despite flying to Moscow from Stansted Airport we would have to fly back to London Gatwick. Normally this would have been a good thing as we lived closer to Gatwick, but my Dad had parked at Stansted which meant he would have to make another journey across there to pick up his car. I got the train from Gatwick back to my parents in Coulsdon that morning and then drove back to Bournemouth. I had a Business Studies exam the next day and this was **perfect** preparation.

2009 : When in Rome...Or Staying Home

Moscow would prove to be the biggest scar that would make the European Cup Winners star above the Chelsea badge in 2012 shine at its brightest. However, there was still time for a few more wounds to be inflicted before our time would come. The following season in 2009, the disappointment of Moscow fuelled the team towards another final in Rome. After successfully beating Juventus and Liverpool we found ourselves against the team that many considered the best ever; Barcelona. Somehow, we had managed to escape the Nou Camp with a 0-0 draw and it was over to the Stamford Bridge faithful to roar Chelsea into a second consecutive final. One of the greatest Chelsea goals of all time from Michael Essien would see us take an early lead. The game grew old and despite relative domination, we were unable to build on our lead. The referees complete failure to award us one of six penalties added to the overwhelming tension inside the stadium, was there to be a final twist? We all know the answer. Iniesta would equalise in the closing minutes to leave every Chelsea fan stunned by what could only be described as an absolute injustice. There was still time for the referee to ignore one of the six calls for a penalty. Chelsea had been eliminated and the wait would go on. On a personal level the scar would stretch a little further as my Dad and I left the ground feeling naturally inconsolable. It was then he would reveal to me that he had booked flights to Rome (the venue of the final) in the week leading to the game to avoid missing out should we qualify. This undoubtedly made it even more sickening to have suffered ejection from the European Cup in such dramatic fashion.

2010-2011 : A Lion Tamed

2010 and 2011 would again prove to be fruitless in terms of Chelsea's European endeavours. Our *"Special One"* would come back to haunt us with his Inter Milan side, knocking us out at the last sixteen stage in 2010. In 2011 defeat at home to Manchester United in the first leg thanks to a Wayne Rooney goal, would be followed by a lacklustre display and 2-1 defeat at Old Trafford that would see us eliminated in the Quarter finals. It was in that moment that Carlo Ancelotti knew his days at Chelsea were up, even though he had achieved Premier League and FA Cup Glory the season before.

Taking Stock

As a fan going into the 2012 season, it was becoming easier to believe that we weren't meant to see Chelsea win the European Cup any time soon, whether it was luck, poor officiating or the simple fact the other team were better. The belief was draining from the Stamford Bridge fans as it seemed the super powers of Didier Drogba, Frank Lampard and John Terry were following a similar fate.

A heavy dose of rationalisation was in order. It was time for me to take stock and put myself in the shoes of the five year old boy in 1993, simply happy to see his team play. The simple truth is only one team from a group of elite clubs can win the European Cup every year and there are millions of fans around the world desperate to see their club clinch the trophy. Undoubtedly important to us Chelsea fans, but not a reason for complete despair. Other clubs and their fans have experienced worse, like relegation, no success, or administration. Just be happy that you have the privilege of seeing your team playing in European competition, an achievement that some fans can only dream of.

2012: Once in a Lifetime Rollercoaster

With feet firmly grounded, and back at the departure lounge, it was time for the 2012 European Champions Rollercoaster to leave the station, with few thoughts of it ending amongst the stars. With seven points from the opening three games of the group stage, it would seem we would successfully navigate a group featuring Bayer Leverkusen and Valencia. However, a draw and a defeat in the next two games would create something of a final in the last group game. Nothing less than a win would be enough in the game against Valencia who held a point advantage, a draw for them would have been enough to knock Chelsea out. Didier Drogba would prove to be the hero with two goals in a 3-0 win to ensure we would proceed to the last sixteen ahead of the Spanish Club.

Last 16: Napoli Vs. Chelsea

An unsettled group stage, left little in terms of renewed expectation for Chelsea fans. Results domestically left a feeling of uncertainty that was becoming all too familiar and wasn't an ideal backdrop to a last 16 clash with a Napoli side featuring a red hot Edison Cavani amongst many other stand out players. It was new territory for Chelsea as in the previous eight seasons we were probably viewed as one of the most dangerous opponents, in 2012 we had lost the fear factor and went in to the knockout stages as underdogs.

A heavy 3-1 defeat away to Napoli left Chelsea fans feeling as if this dog was on the brink of being put down. A surgical procedure was required and Manager Andre Villas Boas would lose his job. Chelsea Legend Roberto Di-Matteo was handed the impossible task of returning the old dog back to a clean bill of health and given the suffering endured out in Napoli it would seem that we would need to suffer more pain before the roar of the Stamford Bridge faithful would be heard again.

Instead, the home leg against Napoli would deliver one of the most incredible nights of football at Stamford Bridge. A goal either side of half time, the first from Didier Drogba and the second from John Terry would put us in the lead on aggregate, but a second goal from Napoli swung the tie back in their favour. Enter Frank Lampard to score the penalty to take the tie in to extra time. The three heroes of the past decade had restored belief once again. An extra time stunner from Ivanovic, brilliantly assisted by Drogba would seal the unlikeliest of qualifications to the quarter finals. An almighty roar could be heard from Stamford Bridge that night as our team showed we wouldn't go down without a fight.

I remember how strange it felt after that game, walking back to the car with my Dad and taking stock of how the evening had unravelled. The outpouring of emotions in the stands was a reflection of the seasons events to date and how amazing it was to clinch victory from the jaws of defeat. From the excitement on the pitch and in the stadium it seemed like we had won the trophy. The truth is we had reached the quarter finals, a place we had been before. Chelsea fans were all too aware the war was far from over after several seasons of experiencing the punishing nature of playing in the Champions League. So despite feeling incredibly happy, having arrived at the game prepared for elimination this was perhaps nothing more than they eye of the storm. We couldn't dream to proceed much further, could we?

Quarter Final: Benfica Vs. Chelsea

Our reward for beating Napoli would be a Quarter final against Benfica. Of all the sides to face, Chelsea fans were undoubtedly happy. At least I was, with only a minor concerns over complacency creeping in as Benfica were considered to be an easier opponent. I'm sure they felt the same about us to be honest, given the alternatives (Bayern Munich, Milan, Barelona and Real Madrid) A 1-0 away win would put us in a strong position, going into the home leg at the Bridge. It would seem we wouldn't need to repeat the heroics we saw against Napoli. Despite taking the lead at the Bridge we allowed them to equalise and sustained heavy pressure as the game drew to a close. Thankfully, as they threw everything at us holes were left in their defence allowing Raul Mirallas to run clear and score emphatically to seal victory and provide passage to another Champions League semi final. Not even a smashed rear car window and a stolen bag could the smile off my face during the drive back from Stamford Bridge to Bournemouth that night.

In recollection the home leg against Benfica was a sloppy display and it was hard to hide the realist in me when it came to our prospects for winning the trophy. Chelsea fans were hiding too many emotional scars from European football to get too carried away. Let's just enjoy the ride while it lasted.

Semi: Chelsea vs. Barcelona

With that in mind it was important to take stock again heading into another Champions League Semi Final. Take a moment to appreciate the fact that we had got that far given the state of play weeks before and how we had just thumped Tottenham 5-1 to reach the FA Cup Final. It felt even more important to take stock, especially as we were due to face the world's best team, featuring the world's best player. It would take a whole lot more than luck to beat a Barcelona side featuring Lionel Messi, Andreas Iniesta, Xavi and Co. Let's not forget Barcelona had dispatched Bayer Leverkusen 10-2 on aggregate in the earlier knock-out stages. A team we had lost to in the group stage.

I'm not sure if I've ever gritted my teeth as much as I did that night at Stamford Bridge. For what seemed like an eternity we were on the back foot and a Barcelona goal seemed inevitable. Somehow despite immense pressure for the entire game, shots off cross bars and countless near misses we would head to the Nou Camp with a 1-0 advantage thanks to a quick fire counter goal from Didier Drogba before half time. How we won that game still baffles me, but Stamford Bridge didn't care. The place was absolutely rocking having endured and defeated such a formidable force.

Despite glimmers of belief there was the small matter of going to the Nou Camp and keeping a prolific Barcelona team at bay. Losing your captain early on and giving away two goals suggested our Champions League run would come to an end. Watching at home it was hard not imagine anything but more goals for Barcelona. Ten men against eleven superstars, in front of 90,000 of their fans, surely this was just a matter of damage limitation. Whether it was the loss of John Terry that inspired the team, but out of nowhere Ramires unleashed a sublime on the run chip from outside the area to pull a goal back before half time, and put us ahead in the tie.

If I still had any teeth left following the home leg at Stamford Bridge the second half in Barcelona would ensure the remainder would be lost within the next 45 minutes. Ramires' ray of hope in the first half seemed to be short lived as we gave away an early penalty. Incredibly Lionel Messi hit the bar and missed. This is the moment Chelsea fans started to wonder again *"is it our year?"*, quickly followed by thoughts or even chants of *"we've seen it before"*.

That half was the best defensive display I have ever seen, given the calibre of opposition, the stage it was on and the fact we only had ten men. The way we thwarted wave after wave of attacks was unreal, as the minutes crawled passed I kept saying to myself how amazing this team has done to get this far, a timely dose of taking stock to prepare the mind for the inevitable Barcelona goal. It was backs against the walls, heart in the mouths as the clocked trickled into the final minutes. The mind was wrestling images of Iniesta's last minute goal in 2009. Under intense pressure an Ashley Cole clearance would provide a few seconds of reprieve, every Chelsea fan expecting the ball to be sucked back towards our goal. Strangely, there was no Barcelona players in sight to pick up the clearance. Instead Fernando Torres had the ball at his feet, running, galloping like a gazelle across the Nou Camp turf, hopping round the goalkeeper, and then I screamed the loudest I have screamed in my front room as the ball hit the back of the net. Chelsea were in another Champions League final. **Chelsea were in another Champions League Final.** That statement required repeating. I remember getting straight on the phone to my Dad and we just had a nutty moment of happiness, both of us pretty delirious, followed by full focus on getting to that game, both ready to re-engage the potential disappointment or highest of highs that might follow.

19.05.2012 : Champions League Final Munich

Thankfully, my dad and I found ourselves in sunny Munich on 19th May 2012. The weather a stark contrast to the grey and gloom in Moscow four years previously. A beautiful, clean, friendly city, full of Bayern Munich fans who were already celebrating their teams win in the sunshine like it was some Tour de France procession. That was genuinely how it felt, every Munich fan had 100% belief the trophy already had their name on it. Chelsea were a spent force who had finished sixth in their league and had no chance of winning, Bayern Munich had stormed to another Bundesliga title and scored *just* fourteen goals in the knockout stage alone. This would be made even more apparent later as the fans inside the Stadium displayed a massive banner that in German read *"Our City, Our Stadium, Our Trophy"*.

Bayern Munich aside, I felt like there was so much at stake. The two weeks leading up to that game I found my mind slipping into every outcome that may occur, simply to help deal with the consequences when they happened. Whilst walking round the fan parks in Munich, I was genuinely thinking this was the last chance my Dad would ever get to see Chelsea win the European Cup. Yes, the after match thoughts of Moscow 2008 had been allowed to creep back in. Champions League qualification for the next season and the clubs glory was of little concern, I just wanted Chelsea to win it for him. After the disappointment in Moscow and everything he had put into taking us to games since 1993 amounted to this one game. That's a pretty desperate thought to have I know, but that's how important it was to share Chelsea's first European Cup glory with him. Chelsea isn't Chelsea without my Dad around.

MIA for 87 Minutes

For 87 minutes of the match Chelsea were Missing In Action. I remember thinking we've got this far and not even turned up. All the hopes and scars we dared to re-open were about to become even wider as these new wounds bled into Moscow's memory. This group of players, the Lampards, Drogba's, Cech's who had risen time and again would finally be snuffed out. Another collection of *"what might have been"* memories when it came to the Champions League.

Incredibly in a game where it seemed like we had barely had a kick we won a corner. Juan Mata would swing it in and Didier Drogba like a superhero emblazoned in blue would glide across the six yard box and smash the ball home with his head. The vastly outnumbered Chelsea fans were in absolute raptures, the man for the big moment had risen once more and equalised right in front of us. Incredible, we had somehow got through to extra time.

Extra Time

I remember looking around during the short interval before the start of extra time and you could see how emotionally drained everyone was. Just coping, just hoping for another miracle. *"Don't worry about a thing"* by Bob Marley was being sung by Chelsea fans as it became apparent that other fans were taking stock of the situation or simply just finding the best way to deal with the tension. Every Chelsea fan knows how extra time unfolded, a feeling of deja-vu kicked in the second Didier Drogba clumsily tripped Ribery in our penalty area to concede a penalty kick. Although the circumstances were different, it would seem Drogba would be cast as the villain as he had done in Moscow 2008. Thankfully, the scriptwriters would have a last minute change of heart. This was to be the moment that the superhero spotlight would switch to Petr Cech as he managed to keep Robben's spot kick out and clutch the ball like his life depended on it. The penalty was taken in front of us and the save brought a roar reminiscent of a full volume Stamford Bridge. A dose of new found belief had been injected into Chelsea fans hearts as penalties loomed eerily on the horizon.

Penalties

Penalties would arrive with a wave of inevitability. The memories of the Moscow penalty shoot out were in every Chelsea fans mind, but light years from the lips. This was no time to fuel the negative thoughts we all shared. Negativity didn't need any encouragement, with a stadium packed full of roaring Munich fans at their backs this was not the place to be wearing blue to take a penalty. Juan Mata would fall victim to the Munich taunts with our first penalty. Chelsea heads were in hands as Munich goalkeeper Neuer effortlessly kept his penalty out, on that showing it would appear we would go out with a whimper. Thankfully the response was different, instead of whimpers the penalties that followed were intense roars of the net bulging from a successful penalty from a hero in blue. In Hollywood fashion Petr Cech would emerge once again to claw away two of Munich penalties and leave 50,000 Bayern fans on the brink of silence.

In this moment I didn't know where to look, watching Didier Drogba walk up to the spot and laying down the ball wasn't a choice, looking at my Dad wasn't either. I was little more than the boy from 1993 who didn't know what to do. I caught a glimpse of him out the corner of my eye and his eyes were locked on a forward position, he couldn't look at me either. The mind was losing a battle against images of John Terry's slip four years previously, there was no time for words. The moment Drogba took two short strides back seemed like an eternity, I can still feel myself standing there helpless on the threshold of a dream. Two steps later and an effortless swing of the right foot. The ball hit the back of the net. Momentary silence. Then a roar so loud, it still ripples through my entire body every time I think about it. Every single time.

CHELSEA HAVE WON THE EUROPEAN CUP!!!

On cue, all 10,000 Chelsea fans in the Allianz Arena went berserk, shredding tears of joy and happiness, flags waving and shirts being hurled into the air. To be there when Chelsea won the European Cup for the first time was an experience that would never be equalled. In amongst it all I grabbed my Dad, tears in my eyes and shouted in his ear "*I love you man!*". That is one of the most incredible moments of my life.

2012

www.throwbackblues.com

MORE THAN A GAME

Reflecting on and writing about my experiences at Stamford Bridge, it's clear that these experiences offer more than meets the eye. There's more to each game and goal than twenty two men kicking a ball around for 90 minutes.. There is a journey or a back story that is either personal to each supporter or associated with the club that is attached to each game, goal or celebration that makes them so special. The memories with my Dad and Grandad amongst other things have shaped my choices in this book. Other Chelsea fans will have their own unique reasons why a specific game is special to them. It's not always a case of these are the best games because we scored the most goals, or it was against this team. Of course these factors can impact the emotions, but sometimes there are other reasons altogether that make them even more special. We attach that moment to where we are in life at that point and that strengthens our memory and fondness for it as it enables us hold on to the things we value the most in life. Football is a fast paced theatre experience, that we can use as a template to manage our own life expectations. The hero isn't always the victor, sometimes the villain is in control and will cast shadows of negativity, but if we continue to believe, the hero can rise again and bring positivity back. Football serves as a reminder that even though the journey in life can seem rocky, the moments of positivity should be used to energise us through tough situations. To always believe that if we dig deep enough and maintain belief the feeling of success and happiness will come in time. I am grateful not only for what I have experienced as a Chelsea fan, but having learnt the importance of overcoming disappointment by thinking positively for the future and being grateful for what I have. The incredible relationship I have with my Dad, the memories I will be able to share with my kids, that is something far bigger than a football match.

2005 2006
2013 1998 1998
2018 2012 2010
2009 2007 2000 1997

2012

2010 2015 2017

1998 2005 2007 2015

PETE & JIM
25 YEARS
CHELSEA FC

AT STAMFORD BRIDGE SINCE '93

Special Thanks to:

My Wife Hannah,
for supporting and believing in me through all my endeavours.

LIFE SENTENCE AT STAMFORD BRIDGE

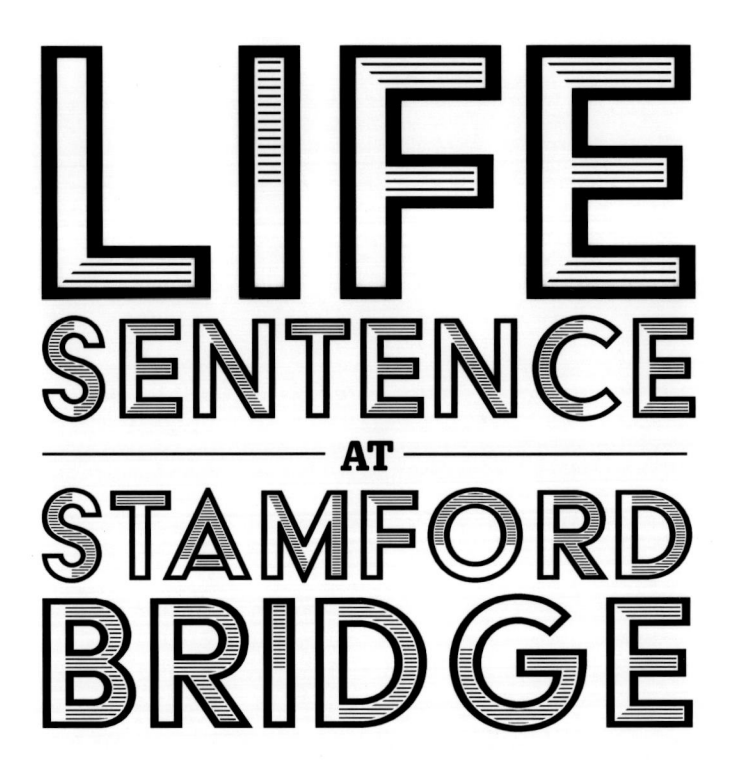

Printed in Great Britain
by Amazon